Project Management
In A Week

Martin Manser is a professional reference book editor. His major projects include leading a team of nearly 100 people to manage one of the few contemporary study bibles (*The Thematic Reference Bible,* Hodder & Stoughton, 1996) to be originated in the UK and leading teams to manage the award-winning *Collins Bible Companion* (HarperCollins, 2009) and the best-selling *Macmillan Student's Dictionary* (Macmillan, 2nd edition, 1996). He is also a Language Trainer and Consultant with national and international companies and organizations, leading courses on project management and business communications.

Website: www.martinmanser.co.uk

I wish to thank Linda Eley for her careful typing of my manuscript.

Project Management In A Week

Martin Manser

Teach Yourself®

First published in Great Britain in 2012 by Hodder & Stoughton. An Hachette UK company.

First published in US in 2012 by The McGraw-Hill Companies, Inc.

This revised, updated edition published in 2016 by John Murray Learning

This edition published in US in 2016 by Quercus

Copyright © Martin H. Manser 2012, 2016

The right of Martin H. Manser to be identified as the Author of the Work has been asserted by him in accordance with the Copyright, Designs and Patents Act 1988.

Database right Hodder & Stoughton (makers)

The Teach Yourself name is a registered trademark of Hachette UK.

British Library Cataloguing in Publication Data: a catalogue record for this title is available from the British Library.

Library of Congress Catalog Card Number: on file.

Paperback ISBN 978 1 473 61026 2

Ebook ISBN 978 1 444 15975 2

1

Typeset by Cenveo® Publisher Services.

Printed and bound in Great Britain by CPI Group (UK) Ltd., Croydon, CR0 4YY.

John Murray Learning policy is to use papers that are natural, renewable and recyclable products and made from wood grown in sustainable forests. The logging and manufacturing processes are expected to conform to the environmental regulations of the country of origin.

John Murray Learning
Carmelite House
50 Victoria Embankment
London EC4Y 0DZ
www.hodder.co.uk

Contents

Introduction

So you have been asked to manage a project. How do you feel? Nervous? Anxious? Excited? Are you wondering where to begin? If you are feeling overwhelmed by the sheer magnitude of the challenge ahead of you, help is at hand. It is right in front of you now, in this guide, which will help you come to grips with the basics of project management in a week.

By the end of the week you will know your way through the process more clearly. For a start, you will have to consult your end users to work out their precise requirements. You will then need to work out the best way to deliver the required outputs, consider the size of the team you will need to meet those requirements and prepare a schedule for the project. Most importantly, you will need to firm up costs, work out a budget and develop monitoring procedures to keep to the agreed costs. You will learn tips for communicating well, especially when dealing with unexpected problems that may arise.

Each day of the week covers a different area and the material is structured for ease of reference. An introduction gives you a 'heads-up' as to what the day is about. The main material then explains the key lessons to be learned. Important principles are clarified and backed up by case studies, quotations and tables. Each day concludes with a summary, next steps and multiple-choice questions, to reinforce the learning points.

I've broken down the subject into easily manageable steps:

Sunday – Think clearly. Lay firm foundations for your project as you clarify and set parameters for the project.

Monday – Plan your project carefully. Begin to make detailed arrangements for the various stages of the project.

Tuesday – Cost your project wisely in the planning stage and ensure that you have rigorous controls in place to monitor costs and quality as you implement the project.

Wednesday – Implement your project successfully. After all your planning and preparation, you are now ready to put the project into practice.

Thursday – Communicate effectively. Good communication with all the colleagues involved in your project is vital to ensure that the team works successfully.

Friday – Deal with change constructively. Here we look at why some projects go off track and how to manage changes.

Saturday – Conclude and evaluate your project positively. How do you complete all the final stages of your project? What lessons can you learn as you evaluate the success of your project?

Finally, at the end of this book is a new '7 × 7' section that offers a distillation of the guidance given in this book, together with some inspirational quotes and resources.

I've written this book to help you make sense of managing a project. If you are new to project management, then this book is for you. If you want to refresh your skills, then this will be a quick-reference guide.

Many other more detailed guides to project management are available, but there are not so many that will help you come to grips with the basics in one week.

I wish you all the best in managing the project before you.

Martin Manser

SUNDAY

Think clearly

Rather than press ahead and dive straight into the action, it is important first to stop and think. Today you will learn how to clear the ground and plan a project, before you put the project into action.

Today we will look at the following aspects of project management:

1 **What is a project?** We will define a project.

2 **Starting a project.** We will consider the basics of beginning a project and offer a creative way for you to develop this for yourself.

3 **Assembling a project team.** We will discuss the colleagues who will help make the project a reality.

4 **Clarifying the project.** We move on from the initial broad parameters to define the project's scope of work, a statement of the project's objectives and outcomes.

5 **What makes a good project manager?** We will look at the qualities you need to be effective.

All this is important to set the scene and to break down the possibly daunting task of being a project manager into more manageable parts.

> *'What is the hardest task in the world?*
> *To think.'*
> Ralph Waldo Emerson, US poet, essayist and philosopher

What is a project?

We can define a project as 'a scheme within a certain time frame that is intended to fulfil a definite purpose. A project needs careful planning and concentrated effort by a group of people.'
Let's break this definition down into its different parts.
A project:

- **is a scheme**: it is a unique and clear plan or enterprise
- **fulfils a definite purpose**: a project is designed to achieve particular aims that are specified
- **is undertaken within a certain time frame**: the project has a schedule with definite and agreed start and end dates
- **needs careful planning**: organized preparation for the project in terms of resources such as money and personnel is vital
- **is undertaken by a group of people**: a project is carried out not by an individual but by many people
- **needs concentrated effort**: completing a project is hard work!

TIP *When planning a project, you will need to specify the following: the number of people included; the financial resources needed; the schedule with milestones; a statement on how you will measure the quality of your output; the equipment and facilities required; and what your final output is.*

Examples of projects

- Update a new computer system
- Build a new school
- Renovate a community centre
- Compile a new reference book
- Arrange and run a conference for 100 participants
- Update a website
- Train your staff in new work procedures
- Restructure a local authority to perform more effectively

Starting a project

What steps do you need to consider as you start a project?

1 **Clarify the idea.** Refine precisely what you are trying to do. Define your aims. It is essential to be clear about what your objectives are.
2 **Make sure you have the agreement of senior management** to your aims, objectives, outcomes and all the resources needed. This may involve carrying out a feasibility study to make sure that the project is sound.
3 **Assess risks.** It is important to identify and manage risks so that the threats of possible risks are minimized. Uncertain events could prevent your project from being carried out successfully. For example:
   - Is the authority of the project leader clear?
   - Is the schedule realistic?
   - Have sufficient financial resources been made available?
4 **Make a business case.** If the project is feasible, you should state the expected benefits that the project would bring against the likely cost. Senior management can then consider the business case and approve the project.

One good way of helping you start thinking about a project is to draw a pattern diagram (also known as a mind map or spider diagram). Take a blank piece of A4 paper. Arrange it in landscape position and write the name of the project in the middle. (Write a word or few words, but not a whole sentence.) You may find it helpful to work in pencil, as you can rub out what you write if necessary.

Now write around your central word(s) the different key aspects of the project that come to your mind. You do not need to list ideas in order of importance; simply write them down. To begin with, you do not need to join the ideas up with lines linking connected items.

If you get stuck at any point, ask yourself the question words *why*, *how*, *what*, *who*, *when*, *where*, and *how much*. These may well set you thinking.

When I do this, I am often amazed at:

● how easy the task is: it doesn't feel like work! The ideas and concepts seem to flow naturally and spontaneously
● how valuable that piece of paper is. I have captured all (or at least some or many) of the key points. I don't want to lose that piece of paper!

Below is an example of a pattern diagram for a project to prepare a new website:

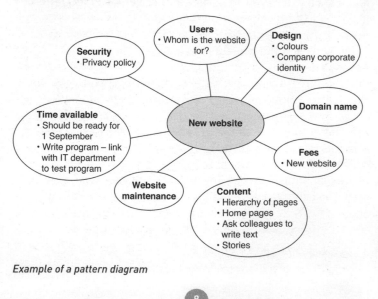

Example of a pattern diagram

Assembling a project team

At an early stage in the project-planning process, you need to gather together the following people in a project team. The purpose of this is to ensure that the preparation is undertaken well. The people or organizations with a strong interest in the outcome of a project are called its **stakeholders**.

Circulate a list of everyone in the project team to the stakeholders, showing their names, job title, contact details (phone, mobile, email, fax).

Project sponsor: a senior member of staff, such as a director of a company or an organization, who can prove that the costs and benefits of the project are worth while. He or she will also need to convince other colleagues in the company or organization that the project is important enough to pursue, given the time and resources being spent on it. He or she will have the authority to reach decisions and approve the spending of the required money and other resources.

Case study: Working efficiently

Dick, as Director, was asked to consider the feasibility of updating his company's computer systems. The company had recently taken on a smaller firm and each company had its own system. The result was that staff were spending too much time inputting the same data in different computer fields.

Dick knew that it made sense to update the smaller firm's systems, but he wondered whether it was also worth updating all the systems for the whole company at the same time that the two systems were being merged. He compared the costs of updating the smaller firm's systems with the cost of updating the whole new merged system. He calculated that, given the likely need to update the (larger) company's software within a year anyway, it made financial sense to update all the merged company's systems at one time. So Dick became project sponsor and assembled colleagues to work with him on the project of updating the company's computer systems.

SUNDAY
MONDAY
TUESDAY
WEDNESDAY
THURSDAY
FRIDAY
SATURDAY

Project manager: the person who reports to the project sponsor and is responsible for implementing the project. The project sponsor should give the project manager the responsibility and authority to carry out the project.

Team members: the project manager, in liaison with the project sponsor, can delegate tasks to members of the team. The project manager delegates to skilled team members whom he or she can trust to get on with the tasks delegated. If they are less experienced, the project manager will need to train, monitor and supervise the colleagues more.

Users (or customers): the people who will use the end result of the project. It is important not merely to consult such people but to understand their needs and involve them in the project so that they feel a valued part of the decision-making process.

Suppliers: the people who carry out certain tasks in the project. Such colleagues may be within or outside your company or organization. Examples are colleagues working in departments that deal with sales, accounts or computers. Suppliers will ensure that the requirements of the project are met, given the time and financial resources agreed.

TIP *As you lay the foundations for the project, spend time building good working relationships with the key colleagues you will be working with. That will be very useful to you if you face difficulties later in the project.*

Organizing your team

If your project is large, you will probably split the organizing of the team and its stakeholders into two different groups:

● **the steering committee** (or **project board**)
This comprises the project sponsor, the project manager and representatives of users and representatives of suppliers. The role of the steering committee is to ensure that the business case is feasible, that the project's end result is usable and that it is practicable, given the required supplies.

● **the project team**
This comprises the project manager and key colleagues who will actually carry out the project's tasks, or – if the project team is large – representatives of such colleagues. However you organize your team, it is important to clarify and agree the roles, responsibilities and authority of each person.

Case study: Renovating a community centre

Smithshire Council wants to renovate a community centre on the Doverville housing estate. The Council wants to involve the residents of the estate and see that they participate fully in the project. The residents, being the users of the project, want to understand the benefits the project will bring.

Doverville residents want their say on a range of matters: the activities planned; the running costs; their involvement in the ongoing running of the centre; how to deal with risks such as vandalism; the overall timetable of the renovation; and where community groups will meet during the renovation.

The Smithshire councillors – who are responsible for authorizing the project's go-ahead and for paying the costs of renovation – want to listen to residents' opinions rather than impose their own views. In this way, by involving the users from the outset, the project is well planned.

SUNDAY
MONDAY
TUESDAY
WEDNESDAY
THURSDAY
FRIDAY
SATURDAY

Clarifying the project

Once you have gathered all the key members of your project team, you will need to hold an initial meeting to discuss the broad parameters of the project. The purpose here is not to go into detail (which will follow later), but to gather information around key areas.

Ideally, the project sponsor would chair this initial meeting, and would begin the meeting by clarifying the reasons why such a project was significant at that time.

Examples of matters to be discussed at this initial meeting could include the following. (Note that it is important to record the points discussed and agreed.)

● **context**
What needs is the project intended to satisfy? How has the present situation developed? How does the project align with the company's or organization's overall strategy?

● **schedule**
What is the project's timescale? When can it begin? By when does it need to be completed? Is the end date critical? For example, if the project is to complete the manufacture of toys for Christmas, they would need to be available for delivery in plenty of time for December.

● **strategy**
Have the needs been identified? What different approaches have been suggested to satisfy those needs? What precisely does the customer want to be delivered?

● **resources**
Has a budget for the project been established? Is there sufficient time to deliver the project? How many members of staff need to be involved? What outside suppliers need to be involved? Have the benefits been analysed against the costs? Where will the project team be located?

● **limitations**
Having defined what you want the project to do, what do you *not* want it to do? For example, if you are updating the financial software of a company, you need to ask to what

extent you want to change your existing bookkeeping and accounting methods. Further, are there legal, security or health and safety requirements that you need to comply with? What risks (uncertain events) can you identify?

The aim here is to produce a document that shows:

- the context of the project: its background
- the aims of the project
- the needs of the customer
- a statement that your project will meet the customer's needs
- the benefits that the project will bring
- the costs of the project and return on investment
- the timescale of the project (start, end and the key intermediate points)
- the human resources needed
- the potential risks of the project.

SMART goals

Your statements of what you are to deliver and the resulting benefits should be SMART, as defined in the following table:

S	**Specific:** not vague but defined precisely
M	**Measurable:** quantifiable so that you can check your progress objectively
A	**Agreed:** to be approved by all involved in the project, that is, the business, users and suppliers
R	**Realistic:** achievable and within reach of the team
T	**Timed:** showing stated dates for start, intermediate stages and for completion

Defining a scope of work

So far we have considered:

- What is a project?
- Starting a project
- Assembling a project team
- Clarifying the project.

It is now time to add further detail to the thinking in order to produce a scope of work and gain approval for the project. Such a scope of work builds on the information that you have already obtained.

A statement of scope of work is also known by other names in companies or organizations. Such names include 'terms of reference' or 'project brief'. If you are in doubt as to the precise contents of the scope of work or its equivalent, check with a senior colleague in your company or organization to find out your policy on such matters.

A statement of the scope of work is important for two reasons:

1 It may well form part of the legal contract between you and outside suppliers. This is important because, if disagreements or disputes arise, the different sides will turn to the contract (scope of work) to read what is stated there about the disputed matter.
2 It provides a definite standard against which progress can be measured.

The scope of work will include statements of:

- **the project's objectives, background, scope and limits** (that is, what the project is and is not going to do)
- **the customers' expectations,** specifying in detail what the project will deliver (for example, the exact type and number of products). It will also include reference to any relevant legal standards that will be complied with
- **the budget** (showing the financial resources needed)
- **a list of other physical resources** (such as new offices, computers)
- **criteria for acceptance** (for example, if I am writing a book, the publisher will make a payment to me only when they consider the work I deliver to be of an acceptable standard)
- a list of the **main colleagues** on the project team
- **delivery dates** for the products
- **assumptions** made about the project; **risks** that could have an effect on the implementation of the project.

A contract will include such a scope of work and specify payments and when payments are to be made (for example,

linked to the delivery of certain products) and other relevant facts (such as patents on products or rights of ownership).

You are now in a position to present your case. You have the results of a feasibility study and a scope of work. The project sponsor will present these at a senior level in order to obtain approval for the project to go ahead.

Prince2®

Prince2 is a method of project management used across a wide range of industries. It provides a framework that covers the different aspects of a project, describing the roles and tasks of stakeholders and ways of monitoring and controlling the project so that the targets of time, cost, quality and benefits are met.

'Project management is the planning, delegating, monitoring and control of all aspects of the project, and the motivation of those involved, to achieve the project objectives within the expected performance targets for time, cost, quality, scope, benefits and risks.'

Prince2 Pocketbook, 2009, page 7

The qualities of a project manager

We end Sunday by considering the qualities of a project manager. The person leading a project – who implements it through to achieving its desired purpose – should be:

- **skilled in leadership:** clear vision and good communication skills are essential
- **a good team leader:** respecting others and focusing on people's strengths
- **good with people:** able to get on with others, to motivate others in a team
- **focused on the goal**
- **good time manager**
- **good motivator**
- **assertive and decisive**
- **committed to the project:** having an active, positive belief in it
- **skilled in management,** with an ability to think strategically, chair meetings well, respect colleagues and lead effectively
- **skilled in negotiation,** to secure win-win situations
- **skilled in delegation** to trusted colleagues, to avoid becoming stressed by taking too much on yourself
- **organized:** someone who is careless or sloppy in their professional life will not be a good project manager
- **highly numerate:** proficient with figures
- someone with **good business sense,** to keep an eye on costs
- someone with **an eye for detail,** who is thorough and meticulous (but see the next quality)
- **able to see the big picture:** someone who sees only details will quickly become overwhelmed and unable to see things in perspective and move forward
- **able to keep track of different processes** (keep several 'balls in the air') at the same time
- **proactive:** able to stay in control and think ahead
- **creative and flexible** in finding solutions to difficulties
- **able to document progress clearly**
- **good at resolving conflict**
- **patient and determined.**

Which qualities do *you* need to cultivate more?

SUNDAY
MONDAY
TUESDAY
WEDNESDAY
THURSDAY
FRIDAY
SATURDAY

Summary

Today we have been concerned with preparation: thinking about and clarifying the parameters of your project. We looked at the first steps we need to take when managing a project, which include making a business case and developing a project brief to gain approval for the project, gathering a project team to begin to make the project work, and understanding the needs of customers. We then looked at how to assess the risks and uncertain situations you may face, before defining the scope of work and working out the schedule for the project. Finally, we considered the essential qualities needed to be a good project manager.

Now take the following practical steps:

1 Summarize the aim of your project in 20 words.

2 Conduct a feasibility study to make a business case to secure approval by senior management.

3 Gather a project team around you.

4 List the main needs of your customers or users.

5 List the main risks that could affect your project.

6 State the key dates in the project's timescale.

7 Consider which qualities of a good project manager you need to cultivate.

MONDAY
TUESDAY
WEDNESDAY
THURSDAY
FRIDAY
SATURDAY

Fact-check [answers at the back]

1. What is a project?
   a) An ongoing role at work ❏
   b) A defined scheme to achieve a particular purpose ❏
   c) A piece of work, e.g. in history at school ❏
   d) The thoughts you think someone else has ❏

2. What does a project need?
   a) Poor motivation ❏
   b) Spontaneity ❏
   c) No planning ❏
   d) Careful planning ❏

3. Gaining the support of senior management for a project is:
   a) Likely ❏
   b) Probable ❏
   c) Essential ❏
   d) Voluntary ❏

4. What is risk assessment?
   a) Taking avoidable risks ❏
   b) Taking unavoidable risks ❏
   c) Knowing how and when things could go wrong ❏
   d) Knowing how and when things could go right ❏

5. What are stakeholders?
   a) The key people included in a project ❏
   b) Those the directors take out to lunch ❏
   c) Only the users of a project ❏
   d) The team members of a project ❏

6. Who is the project sponsor?
   a) Your company's main advertiser ❏
   b) A senior member of staff, e.g. a director, responsible for the project ❏
   c) The person who implements a project ❏
   d) Your customers ❏

7. When formulating a plan, considering your users' needs is:
   a) Unnecessary ❏
   b) A waste of time ❏
   c) Vital ❏
   d) Quite important ❏

8. In SMART goals, what does the S stand for?
   a) Silly ❏
   b) Standard ❏
   c) Special ❏
   d) Specific ❏

9. What must the scope of work include?
   a) Details of what the project will deliver ❏
   b) Details of the times you begin and finish your job ❏
   c) Your informal thoughts on possible risks ❏
   d) An exhaustive list of all the project's stakeholders ❏

10. What does a project manager need to be?
    a) A good speaker ❏
    b) A good organizer ❏
    c) A good loser ❏
    d) A good boss ❏

MONDAY

Plan your project carefully

You've got the go-ahead for the project, and your colleagues congratulate you. You feel on top of the world for a few hours... and then you get a feeling in the pit of your stomach, as fear and anxiety begin to creep in. How can you steer the ship successfully through the waters? What if you fail?

The next step is not to panic but to build on all the thinking you have already undertaken. Today we will look at planning carefully. One of the key qualities we emphasized on Sunday was being organized, and this is where all your organizational skills come into play.

It's important to resist the urge just to get on with the work. Instead, do further preparation. When you decorate a room, for example, most of the work is in preparing the surfaces, stripping off wallpaper and rubbing down the walls before you can start. Similarly, when you had to write an essay at school your teachers encouraged you to create a structure before beginning. You discovered that if you didn't, you would get halfway through it and wonder where you were going. The same applies to managing any project.

What is planning?

Planning is a way in which we can come to grips with something complex and define certain matters in a structured way. Time spent in planning and preparation is time well spent.

As a minimum, you need to define:

- **the separate stages** of a project: **what** needs to be achieved?
- **the resources** needed for each stage:
  - the **personnel** required: **who** is going to undertake the tasks?
  - the **financial resources** needed for each stage: how much is each task going to cost? (See also Tuesday.)
  - **other resources** (such as offices, computers and other equipment) needed
  - **the times** when each stage will happen: **when** will the tasks be done?

The following are also significant:

- the **quality** of what is delivered. A plan does not simply list different stages; all the expectations (see Sunday) must be met. Effective procedures and standards need to be set to keep control of the project (see Tuesday)
- the **risks** (uncertain events) that could affect the successful implementation of the project. The aim therefore is to identify such risks and do all you can to reduce the likelihood of their occurrence.

> *'By failing to prepare, you are preparing to fail.'*
>
> Benjamin Franklin

Case study: Updating an intranet

Betty was put in charge of updating the company's intranet. The company originally set up its intranet some years ago simply by including many of the standard documents that were widely available. The updated intranet needed to be operational within three months. Betty wisely gathered together users from various parts of the company to discuss the project: design, IT departments as well as representatives from each of the areas the company covered. They discussed their ideas and suggestions, dividing the work into three different stages and allocating someone responsible for each of the stages with definite dates given for the completion of each stage. After the meeting she circulated the minutes to each participant. The result was a well-planned basis for the project.

Divide up the work

You know your overall aim, which might be 'to update your website by 1 May' or 'to arrange a conference for mid-October'.

You now need to break down this overall aim into manageable tasks.

When I go on a long-haul flight, I like to keep an eye on the progress. For example, on a 13-hour flight I work out what percentage of the journey I have covered after, say, 45 minutes (6 per cent), 1.5 hours (12 per cent), and so on. Dividing up the overall journey time and measuring progress in a concrete way helps me feel I am on my way to reaching my goal. Similarly, breaking down the overall tasks into smaller, more manageable activities enables us to know where we are in a project.

Analyse the project you defined in your scope of work, as discussed on Sunday, into manageable pieces ('chunks') of work. The name of such an analysis is a **work breakdown structure** (WBS).

For example, you may need to plan a conference with an international speaker for next spring. You could divide the work up into smaller units as follows:

1 Receive project go-ahead.
2 Book speaker.
3 Arrange venue.
4 Arrange accommodation and travel for speaker.
5 Arrange publicity for conference.
6 Receive bookings.
7 Do admin.
8 Produce handouts.
9 Make final checks:
   – check venue will provide projector
   – check speaker will bring laptop with presentation already loaded on.
10 Run conference.
11 Evaluate at end.

Key this information on to a spreadsheet, or use a proprietary software program.

Notice one key point in this list: each item (for example, '2 Book speaker', '3 Arrange venue') consists of a verb (doing word) plus a noun (thing). Normally, when we make a list, we tend to think only of nouns – you probably put nouns in the pattern diagram on Sunday. Adding verbs can be very useful as they express the practical action you need to do: *arrange*, *receive*, *check*, *evaluate*.

If you get stuck at any point, here are two hints:

1 Ask the question words *why*, *how*, *what*, *who*, *when*, *where*, *how much* (look back at Sunday).
2 Begin at the end and work backwards. In other words, start with what you need to deliver or produce and think of the different stages that have to be undertaken to meet that goal.

What you will notice

As you develop this list of tasks, you will notice several things:

- You can further subdivide each task into smaller tasks, so go ahead and do that. Your aim here is to list *every* significant task that needs to be completed. Again, try to write both a verb, such as *identify, assess, collect, review,* and a noun for each task.
- Although your aim is to list all significant tasks, you will not achieve that immediately, so go for successively more exact ('iterative') definitions of what you want to achieve. I remember, for example, sitting down with a computer software developer to define the requirements of handling large amounts of data on a major project I led. It took many meetings to define precisely what I wanted, but we had to start somewhere and work gradually towards the goal of a full specification.
- Each task will require further information, for example about time and personnel resources – the subjects of the other parts of today.
- Some tasks are dependent on other tasks, while other tasks are independent. For example, you need to book a speaker in advance of arranging publicity because you will want to include the speaker's name and credentials on the publicity. On the other hand, booking the speaker and arranging the venue do not depend on each other.

SUNDAY MONDAY TUESDAY WEDNESDAY THURSDAY FRIDAY SATURDAY

TIP **The work breakdown structure**
*Involve the key members of your project in preparing the work breakdown structure. It is not **your** analysis, it is the team's; and it forms a significant part of your records for keeping track of the project. Update the work breakdown structure as you go along.*

Set a timetable

You have now listed the tasks, with many subtasks, and you now need to add further significant information. You can add more columns to your spreadsheet to show the duration of tasks (in working days or hours) and start and end dates, or use a **Gantt chart** (named after the US engineer and management consultant Henry Gantt, 1860–1919). A Gantt chart has the added advantage that it also shows:

- milestones: particular key dates
- who is responsible for different stages.

The critical path

If you list the tasks you need to complete a project, with dates, you will discover the critical path, 'the series of tasks that take the longest time to complete'. Using the example from earlier today, booking a speaker for an international conference is an event on the critical path. If booking a speaker is delayed, you cannot arrange conference publicity that gives his or her name and so you cannot receive bookings. On the other hand, checking that the venue has a projector is a non-critical event: it can be undertaken at any time before the actual event. So we can define a non-critical path as the series of tasks that can be delayed but you would still complete your project in the shortest time.

It is important to note that the length of time taken to complete tasks on the critical path cannot be increased without a significant effect on the schedule.

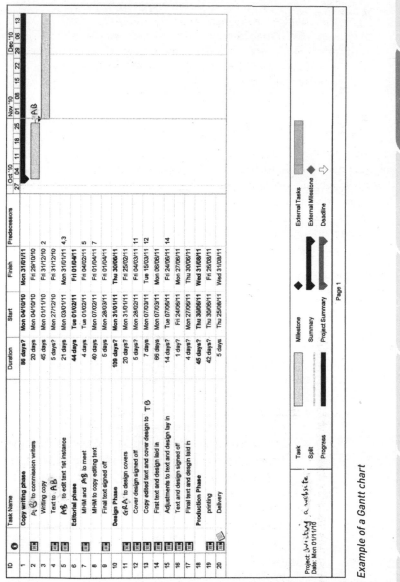

Example of a Gantt chart

Don't forget...

When planning schedules, remember to allow for:

- holidays, both individuals' and public ones
- other work that individuals might undertake at the same time. For example, a colleague might be compiling a report for another department on the days you have allocated for her to be available in your project
- unproductive time. You may sit at your desk from 9 a.m. to 5 p.m. with breaks for lunch, but how much of that time is actually productive?

All these factors need to be remembered. As a rule of thumb, I estimate that I work productively for about 1,500 hours per year. I arrive at this figure as follows:

52 weeks per year
– 4 holidays
– 2 other: sickness, training
= 46 weeks.

I am at my desk 8.30 a.m. – 12.30 p.m., 1.30 p.m. – 5.30 p.m. = 8 hours but I do productive work for only 6.5 hours per day. (The rest is routine admin, development work and checking accounts.) This amounts to 32.5 hours per week. And 46 weeks × 32.5 hours = 1,495 hours.

Allocate people to activities

So far you have listed all the activities in the order in which they need to be undertaken. Your next task is to allocate people to those activities.

List activities and roles

Activity	Role
Book speaker	Director
	Secretary
Arrange venue	Director
	Secretary
Arrange publicity	Head of Marketing
	Head of Design

At this stage, assign roles to the activities. You may well have certain named people in mind, but here it is more important to allocate the activities to a particular job title.

You know exactly how long some activities will take. To travel to a city in another part of the country may take three hours. To fill in certain forms and go through certain procedures may take, say, ten hours. For other activities, the amount of time actually spent will depend on the number of colleagues working on that part of the project. For example, I think I know that to check through 1,000 entries in a computer logging system will take one person four days, that is, he or she will work through 250 per day. If I have four people all doing that same work, the amount of actual time taken will (I think) be one day in duration.

Assign times to activities

We now move on to put figures of timings against the various activities listed. The aim here is not simply to pluck figures out of the air by not giving any thought to the question 'How long do you think that task will take?' but to consider figures as accurately as possible.

If you are unsure about how long an activity takes, try a sample yourself and check the time it takes. Taking the example above, you yourself could actually check 50 records and see how long that takes you. The assumption was 250 entries per day, so you think someone could check 50 entries in one-fifth of a day, based on a seven-hour day (420 minutes) divided by 5 = 84 minutes.

But when you try it yourself, you find it actually takes you two hours (120 minutes). So your original assumption of checking 250 records in a seven-hour day is now extremely inaccurate. Based on your actual work, it would take five times (50 × 5 = 250) × 2 hours = 10 hours = about 1.5 days, rather than the one day you originally thought to work through 250 records.

Some activities may well take considerably longer than you think. For example, you think arranging a venue for a conference may take only an hour, but that will be the time needed when you have chosen the actual location. You may spend several hours investigating venues on the Internet and then two days travelling to various locations in your city to see what each venue has to offer.

One way of noting times is to list both estimated and actual figures. This has the advantage of enabling you to learn from experience on future occasions, when you can look at the actual times taken in contrast to the estimated ones.

List times against activities

Activity	Role	Estimated hours	Actual hours
Book speaker	Director	4 hours	6 hours
	Secretary	10 hours	12 hours
Arrange venue	Director	7 hours	21 hours
	Secretary	16 hours	25 hours
Arrange publicity	Head of Marketing	5 hours	15 hours
	Head of Design	5 hours	15 hours

Case study: Planning well

Pete was in charge of a multi-author report that was to be written by ten directors from various parts of the world. He initially drew up a schedule of delivery dates from the different authors, but realized that to ask the same delivery date for every author would mean that he would end up having to edit ten contributions at the same time.

He worked out therefore that he needed to do one of two things. He either needed to keep those original dates and draw on additional colleagues to help him edit their texts. If he did that, he knew that he would have to allow a few additional hours administering their work, writing briefing notes for his editors, checking their work and answering their queries. Alternatively, he realized he could stagger the delivery dates so that they did not all happen at the same time. By considering the arrangements carefully, Pete ensured that he did not give himself more work than he could cope with at one time.

Allow for contingencies

As well as allowing time for holidays, illness and administration, you need to allow time for:

● **project start-up**
   If you are given the go-ahead on 10 May, it may not be 10 or 11 May that you actually start. You may need to complete other work first. This also applies to induction of new members of staff, briefing colleagues you may outsource work to, installing new computer software and setting up offices.

● **'between times'**
   These are the times between events happening. For example, a factory may deliver 5,000 CDs to a warehouse but it may be one week between the time when they are delivered and the time when they are sent out to distributors. So you need to make allowance for that week. Another example of 'between times' is the time taken between first

drafting a report to when it is approved by the project board or a company's senior management or directors.

- **unplanned events**
Projects often overrun because you have not built in contingency time. Contingency time is time that you include as a necessary part of your overall schedule to allow for unplanned events that could significantly delay your project.

> *'The first 90 per cent of a project takes the first 90 per cent of the time. The last 10 per cent of the project takes the last 90 per cent of the time.'*
>
> Anon.

Managing risks

Risks need to be identified, assessed and then dealt with. The key point to remember is that you will not survive a project without encountering certain risks, so it is better to plan to deal with them rather than be surprised when they unexpectedly arise.

You should prepare a risk-assessment document that lists potential risks, their probability of occurrence, the extent of their effect on your project objectives and your responses to them.

Example of risk assessment for a holiday booking company

Risk	Probability	Effect	Response
Publicity inadequate	Low	Medium	Revise publicity; go to new supplier
Computer software breaks down	Medium	High	Ensure that technicians are available 24/7
Too many bookings	Medium	High	Identify other accommodation
Poor weather	Medium	High	Include holidays with indoor activities

Summary

Today we have been concerned with planning. We have seen how to define a project in a structured way, and how to divide up the work into separate manageable parts to make a work breakdown structure. We then looked at how to set a timetable for the project, remembering to make allowances in the schedule for known events such as project start-up, administration and holidays, and unknown events. We also learned how to allocate people to activities and ways of preparing to manage potential risks.

Now take the following practical steps:

1 Define the different stages of your project in a work breakdown structure.

2 Break down the different stages into smaller, separate pieces of work.

3 Assign a role to each activity and consider how long it will take.

4 Compile a spreadsheet or Gannt chart showing the tasks, roles and times needed for the different tasks.

5 List possible contingencies that could affect your project.

6 Prepare a risk-assessment document for your project.

SUNDAY
MONDAY
TUESDAY
WEDNESDAY
THURSDAY
FRIDAY
SATURDAY

Fact-check [answers at the back]

1. What should you do when you start a project?
   a) Go for it! Just begin ❏
   b) Start with the easiest part ❏
   c) Start with the most difficult part ❏
   d) Plan first ❏

2. What is a work breakdown structure?
   a) A plan when the project breaks down ❏
   b) A plan of the benefits of a project ❏
   c) A plan of the different activities in a project ❏
   d) A plan of the people needed in a project ❏

3. What does a Gannt chart show?
   a) Tasks, duration and colleagues to do the tasks ❏
   b) Only the tasks of the project ❏
   c) Only the duration of the project ❏
   d) Only the key dates in the project ❏

4. When planning, what should you do about interruptions?
   a) Hope no interruptions come ❏
   b) Manage them wisely ❏
   c) Ignore them ❏
   d) Plan for them ❏

5. When planning, what should you do about delays between tasks?
   a) Allow for them ❏
   b) Expect them ❏
   c) Ignore them ❏
   d) Monitor them ❏

6. When compiling a schedule, what should you include?
   a) Time for lunch ❏
   b) Time for holidays ❏
   c) Money spent on office equipment ❏
   d) Staff salaries ❏

7. What is a critical path?
   a) The series of tasks that are unnecessary in the project ❏
   b) The series of tasks that are necessary in the project ❏
   c) The series of tasks that take the longest time to complete ❏
   d) The series of tasks that can be criticized ❏

8. What do contingencies refer to?
   a) Unplanned events that could significantly delay a project ❏
   b) Planned events that could significantly delay the project ❏
   c) Bad weather ❏
   d) Good weather ❏

9. How important is it to allow time for contingencies?
   a) Not important ❏
   b) Helpful but not vital ❏
   c) Important in some cases ❏
   d) Essential ❏

10. How important is compiling a risk assessment?
   a) It's an optional extra ❏
   b) It's a nice-to-have ❏
   c) It's essential ❏
   d) It's useful if you have time to write one ❏

TUESDAY

Cost your project wisely

Yesterday we dealt with overall planning; today we will consider costing as a separate matter because this is a key area in which projects may fail.

How long will the tasks take? How many people will you need to complete your project? Where will you find such people – and how long will it take you to find and brief them, how long to administer and check their work? What about outside suppliers? Will you choose the cheapest or the best? How reliable are they? All these factors, and more, will have a bearing on the cost of your project.

The title of today's chapter deliberately includes the adverb 'wisely' because, for me, wisdom refers to knowledge plus experience. You can gain much useful knowledge from texts such as this one, but until you have applied this knowledge and seen how it works out in experience in actual projects, you won't have gained the wisdom for yourself.

Our overall aim is to deliver quality: this means a high standard of work. Because our discussion of cost is rooted in a desire to produce high-quality products, after considering cost we will go on to consider quality.

Why financial resources are important

Financial resources are significant in project management in two areas:

1 **in the planning stage**, ensuring that your estimates are as precise as possible. This means that they are:
   - accurate, not vague
   - based on measured tasks, that is, ones that can be quantified, not approximate. (Of course, in the planning stage, you cannot be absolutely exact, but your aim should be to be as precise as possible.)
2 **in the implementation stage**, ensuring that your costs are managed and controlled as rigorously as possible. This means:
   - monitoring costs incurred
   - authorizing any additional costs that are necessary.

Costs should be considered at every stage of the project:

1 **in the thinking stage**. This is when you conduct a feasibility study considering the likely costs against the expected benefits in order to make a business case. (See also Sunday.)
2 **in the planning stage.** There are three points here:
   - your preparation of a work breakdown structure (WBS), taking your estimates (which are as precise as possible) of the time each activity will take (see also Monday) and working out the costs from that
   - your calculations of any income that may come into the project (for example, if you are holding a conference, not only will you incur costs such as venue and speakers' costs, you will also receive income from participants)
   - your discussions of contracts. If you are involving outside suppliers, you can assess their offer and evaluate the price they will charge. You should also consider the dates when payments will be made to ensure that you have a good cash flow

3 **in keeping to the project budget.** When you have estimated all your project costs as precisely as possible and confirmed any contracts for outside suppliers, you can gain approval and confirmation of the costs of the project. You can then use such costs as a basis against which actual costs can be compared during the project's implementation and evaluation

4 **in controlling costs** when the project is being implemented. You do not want expenditure to escalate out of control so you need to have in place systems and procedures for tracking expenditure, that is, monitoring costs, analysing any deviations and, where necessary, giving the authority to make additional expenditure

5 **in evaluating the project.** At the end of the project, you can check the final costs against the original estimates and also make sure that the planned return on investment has been met.

'Time is money'

We often say that 'time is money', but what does that mean? Suppose you earn £20,000 per year. If we divide this figure by the number of days you work productively, that is, omitting holidays and allowing for illness, this could give, say, 46 weeks per year, so £20,000 ÷ 46 = £434.78 per week or £86.96 per day, assuming five days per week. If we then divide this figure by the time per day you spend on productive work, say two-thirds of seven hours (= 4.66 hours), we come to £18.66 per hour: this is the amount that you are paid per hour gross (before tax and other deductions).

That is only half the story, however. Your actual cost to your company or organization is about twice that figure once you allow for the overheads of that company: its general business expenses, the taxes it pays as an employer, the rent of the office building, heating, power, water, and so on. The cost to your company or organization is therefore £18.66 × 2 = £37.32 per hour.

If a business meeting lasts seven hours and is attended by six colleagues, the cost of that meeting to the company or organization is 7 × 6 × £37.32 = £1,567.44. No wonder we are asked to make the most of our time!

Work out the cost of your project

For the **work breakdown structure** (WBS), you can now begin to assign costs. As part of that task, you will need to decide who will undertake the work. Will the work be done by:

- you?
- colleagues in your department?
- colleagues in other departments in your company or organization?
- an outside supplier?

For each of the above, you will need to know the hourly (or day) rate of the people concerned. You will also need to check to

what extent company overheads are included if your project is charged to colleagues from another department in your company or organization.

Estimate cost of project

Activity	Role	Estimated hours	Hourly rate £	Estimate £
Book speaker	Director	4 hours	80	320
	Secretary	10 hours	30	300
Arrange venue	Director	7 hours	80	560
	Secretary	16 hours	30	480
Arrange publicity	Head of Marketing	5 hours	60	300
	Head of Design	5 hours	60	300
Total				£2,260

Using outside suppliers

If you decided to outsource to outside suppliers, for example if they have greater expertise than your in-house staff, you will need to brief them on the precise work required. This brief should include such obvious matters as schedule, statement of work required and payment, and also less obvious but important matters such as a statement of the ownership of the work.

For example, if a freelance author is being paid a fee for writing a text, then you should prepare a statement on whether he or she retains ownership of that text and what publishing rights he or she is granting to the company or organization he or she is working for.

Remember to build into your budget:

- time to brief a range of possible suppliers
- time to evaluate their bids and reach a decision on which supplier to choose
- time to brief the supplier at the outset of the work ('start-up' time)
- time to administer and keep track of their work
- an approximate level of contingency to handle risks and other uncertain events that will arise (see Monday).

Case study: Cash-flow problems

Chris was seconded by a communications agency to compile and edit a report on a possible new shopping centre in the north of the UK. He delegated the initial drafting of sections to experts in various fields such as transport, consumer needs and expectations and supermarket trends. He presented the agency with an overall budget of £25,000, which was agreed, but he didn't realize until it was too late that this sum was payable only on completion of his report. He should have planned a cash flow, so that he could cover his own costs and those of his suppliers during the course of the project.

Develop a procurement policy

Procurement is the term used to decide the process by which goods and services are obtained by outside companies or organizations. The following factors should be considered:

- the **authority** of those making decisions on awarding contracts. The colleagues who make decisions on whom to award contracts to should undertake their work with professional integrity and fairness

- the **criteria** on which decisions are made. When evaluating and awarding contracts you should be as objective as possible when comparing price, delivery dates and the financial soundness, reliability and previous experience of the company or organization
- the **terms and conditions** of a contract. As the saying goes, 'The devil is in the detail'. Look at the terms and conditions, especially those concerning delivery of goods and services and dates of payment. If you are uncertain about anything, ask.

Decisions, decisions

As part of your planning, you should decide on the kind of contract you want to offer to an outside supplier. Is it a fixed contract (for example, building a website) or does it involve regular maintenance (for example, maintaining a website or providing security in an office building)?

If you are considering using a supplier you have not worked with before, visit their offices and get to know their staff, and/or ask for references from previous companies or organizations that have used their services before. Do not simply rely on their website.

Making a good return on investment

Return on investment is the percentage return you make over a certain time as a result of undertaking the project. It is calculated according to the formula:

ROI = (profits [or benefits] ÷ investment [your costs]) × 100

One way of considering return on investment is to work out the **payback** period, the time taken for the profits or benefits to cover the cost of your investment.

For example, a project to train your staff in report-writing skills might cost £50,000, including fee for tutor, materials and administration. If its benefits could be measured in terms of savings of work time and productivity increases of £60,000 over one year, the return on investment would be (60,000 ÷ 50,000) × 100 = 120%.

SUNDAY MONDAY TUESDAY WEDNESDAY THURSDAY FRIDAY SATURDAY

Finalize the project budget

Make sure that you have included the cost of:

- **colleagues:** the time spent by your colleagues, colleagues in other departments, colleagues in outside companies or organizations, including start-up and administration time
- **equipment or facilities** needed for the project, such as computers or offices
- **other human-resource costs** such as recruitment and training
- **other departments' costs** such as IT and marketing.

Your budget should also include:

- cash-flow predictions during the whole of your project
- any income forecasts that are part of the project
- the 'cost centres' to which particular items of expenditure will be allocated during the implementation of the project
- contingency: a figure of about 10 per cent of your total costs is often suggested.

Example of extract of a budget for a training course

	Costs
Speaker	4,000
Venue	6,000
Marketing	3,000
Administration	2,000
Office	2,000
Contigency	2,000
Total	19,000
	Income
Delegates' fees	22,000
Profit	**3,000**

Why quality is important

So far today, we have considered the role of financial resources and their significance at every stage of a project (planning, implementation and evaluation). However, while keeping to your budget is a vital part of project management, it is by no means the whole story. As the following example shows, accepting low standards of quality results in more work: if you accept work of a poor standard, you will have to unravel all the difficulties caused. You will lose valuable time and delay the project.

Case study: Accepting low-quality standards

Jane asked the company Quality Computers Ltd to install new computer systems in her organization. All went quite well in the planning stage, and the computers were delivered on time and within budget. Unfortunately, only half of them actually worked properly, and as a result Jane had to spend extra time putting matters right. She had not factored in the inconvenience and significant loss of productivity incurred – nor all the additional resources required.

'Accepting low standards of quality results in more work.'

How can you achieve quality in your project?

Here are some practical tips:

- **Make quality something you can measure.**
  'Quality' can be a vague term and it can mean different things to different people. This is why you need to define specific objective criteria by which to measure quality.

- **Be concerned with the customers'/users' requirements.**
  They are the ones for whom you are managing the project and who receive its end result. If matters come to a disagreement, what are the non-negotiable aspects that the customer *must* have?

- **Focus on what is delivered rather than on the process of how you achieve that end.**
  For example, I was recently in charge of a project to deliver 5,000 books to an exhibition in the UK in March. We delivered the text to the printers on schedule in October, but were delayed by packaging difficulties, which meant that with shipping time the books would not reach the UK until April. We therefore had to send the books by air freight to meet the March deadline. The result: a satisfied customer: we delivered what we said we would. We focused on fulfilling the customers' expectations, even though we incurred higher costs of air freight.

- **Build in quality reviews at every stage.**
  Quality isn't a 'nice-to-have': it's an essential. Discuss and agree how quality can be measured objectively regularly through the project.

> *'Quality isn't a "nice-to-have":*
> *it's an essential.'*

- **Ensure that skilled and experienced colleagues conduct the reviews.**
- **Put effective procedures in place that report on quality of performance.**
  If necessary, improve your working methods during the project.
- **Where necessary, include outside consultants to review quality and follow best practice within your industry.**
  For example, on one project I led, all was going technically well internally with a project until a meeting with outside consultants reviewed our work and criticized it for being below standard. We had to reassess our working methods to put the project back on track. Outside consultants have the advantage of not knowing the internal politics of your workplace and they can see directly into a situation that you might for different reasons be unaware of.
- **Do your best _now_.**
  All this talk of quality can seem abstract. It is up to each one of us to do our best with the work that we have to do right in front of us now. We may play only a small part in a large organization but it is our responsibility to produce quality work now, rather than think 'I can't be bothered' and have to sort out problems in a few weeks' or months' time.

ISO 9000

'The ISO 9000 family of standards represents an international consensus on good-quality management practices. It consists of standards and guidelines relating to quality management systems and related supporting standards.'

International Organization for Standardization website:
http://www.iso.org/iso/home.html

Case study: Something wasn't quite right

From the first meeting, Harry knew something wasn't quite right with the outside supplier, Special Solutions Ltd. Harry's company had accepted the lowest bid and Harry was left to manage the project. When he met regularly with colleagues from Special Solutions, they were pleasant enough – in fact, at times they were too pleasant: it was as if their superficial pleasantness was hiding something below the surface. Sure enough, matters came to a head at the second monthly review meeting, when it became clear that Special Solutions had not met their targets for manufacturing and were waiting for one of their suppliers to deliver machines.

The whole matter left Harry with a bad taste in his mouth. Not only did Harry's company have to negotiate a withdrawal from their contract with Special Solutions but they also had to put the contract out for tender again and several months' valuable time was lost. Never again would his company accept a bid simply because it offered the lowest price.

Summary

Today we have been concerned with costing and quality. We have looked at how to cost your project wisely and explained the procedures you need to have in place for monitoring your costs during the implementation of your project. We also learned how to set up cost centres to which you allocate expenditure during the project, as well as ways to avoid cash-flow problems. We also learned how to develop a sound procurement policy that will enable you to produce quality products that meet your customers' requirements, and we outlined the procedures needed for monitoring the quality of your project output.

Now take the following practical steps:

1 Work out the hourly rate that you and the main colleagues involved in the project *actually cost* your company or organization.

2 Cost the different stages of your project that you identified in your work breakdown structure.

3 Prepare a cash-flow forecast for your project.

4 Work out the return on investment given a certain payback period.

5 Finalize your project budget.

6 State precisely the quality of what your project will deliver and how you will measure it.

SUNDAY
MONDAY
TUESDAY
WEDNESDAY
THURSDAY
FRIDAY
SATURDAY

Fact-check [answers at the back]

1. Is it ever possible to run a project successfully without thinking about finance?
   a) Yes, sometimes ❏
   b) Not usually ❏
   c) No, never ❏
   d) Always ❏

2. What should your project budget be?
   a) As cool as possible ❏
   b) As futuristic as possible ❏
   c) As flexible as possible ❏
   d) As exact as possible ❏

3. What do overheads include?
   a) Business costs that you incur in that project ❏
   b) The profit you hope to make ❏
   c) The bridges near your office ❏
   d) General business expenses such as rent, heating and taxes ❏

4. How important is it to consider the cash flow of a project?
   a) It's useful but not vital ❏
   b) It's essential ❏
   c) It's helpful if you have time ❏
   d) It's unnecessary ❏

5. How important is it to include projected income in your budget?
   a) It's helpful if you have time ❏
   b) It's a waste of time ❏
   c) It's unimportant ❏
   d) It's essential ❏

6. What does a procurement policy cover?
   a) Outside leisure time ❏
   b) Outside suppliers ❏
   c) Outside roofs ❏
   d) Outside business contacts ❏

7. How is a return on investment calculated?
   a) ROI = (profits × investment) ❏
   b) ROI = (profits × investment) × 100 ❏
   c) ROI = (profits ÷ investment) × 100 ❏
   d) ROI = (break-even point × investment) × 100 ❏

8. What is the definition of the payback?
   a) The cash you receive at the end of a project ❏
   b) The money needed when you make a loss on a project ❏
   c) The time needed for the benefits to cover the cost of your investment ❏
   d) The money needed as a deposit on a project ❏

9. What is a cost centre?
   a) A unit to which items of expenditure are allocated in a project ❏
   b) A supermarket that sells good-quality food ❏
   c) A unit of profit ❏
   d) A measure of the company's overheads ❏

10. What does ISO 9000 deal with?
    a) Managing people ❏
    b) Managing quality ❏
    c) Managing costs ❏
    d) Managing a project ❏

WEDNESDAY

Implement your project successfully

You have now done all your thinking and preparing. You have finalized your budget and your project proposal and other plans, and you are now ready to go. Do you now just sit back and let things happen, taking their own course?

Today you will learn what you need to do to make sure the project moves ahead efficiently towards a successful conclusion and completion. After all, you have put in a lot of hard work laying firm foundations and certainly you don't want to see them wasted.

We will consider the steps you need to take to move your project forward, building on all your careful preparation, ensuring that you put and keep in place effective control mechanisms to monitor the project's actual schedule and expenditure against what you planned for earlier. You will learn what actions you will need to carry out regularly to keep your project on track. We will also look at how to deal with unforeseen risks and difficulties that can easily arise during your project's implementation stage.

Confirm commitments

As you launch your project, you would be wise to confirm key commitments of:

- **the main people concerned with running the project**
  Check that they all can start on a certain date or as soon as possible after that time.

- **the other stakeholders**
  It is best not to assume that they are fully in the picture: communicate with them the status of the project.

- **the available financial resources**
  You and your colleagues will want to be paid properly, and you need to ensure that any outside suppliers are paid punctually.

Put in it writing

Make sure that you have confirmed in writing the availability, roles, responsibilities and authority of the key stakeholders. It is particularly important to define the activities that each colleague needs to undertake. Look at your **work breakdown structure** and make sure that it defines:

- the work to be undertaken
- the start and end dates

- key milestones, for example:
  - when certain proportions of the work – such as a quarter, half, three-quarters – are completed
  - when a certain level of income has been achieved
  - when a certain output has been delivered and accepted by the customer/user
  - timing of expenditure (costs) and any income received.

The project initiation document (PID)

Prince2® specifies project initiation documentation:

'The purpose of the Project Initiation Documentation is to define the project, to form the basis for its management and the assessment of overall success. The Project Initiation Documentation gives the direction and scope of the project and (along with the Stage Plan) forms the "contract" between the project manager and the project board.

The three primary uses of the Project Initiation Documentation are to:

1 ensure that the project has a sound basis before asking the project board to make any major commitment to the project

2 act as a baseline against which the project board and project manager can assess progress, issues and ongoing viability questions

3 provide a single source of reference about the project so that people joining the "temporary organization" can quickly and easily find out what the project is about, and how it is being managed.

The Project Initiation Documentation is a living product in that it should always reflect the current status, plans and controls of the project. Its component products will need to be updated and re-baselined, as necessary; at the end of each stage, to reflect the current status of its constituent parts.'

(*Prince2 Pocketbook*, 2009, pages 46–7)

Track, control, report

The key aspects of managing a project during its implementation are tracking, controlling and reporting:

● **tracking**

You need to have in place procedures to monitor actual progress against what you had planned. This is so that you can be aware of any slippages or delays as soon as possible so that you can inform your customer of a possibly later delivery date

● **controlling changes**

Any changes that you have recorded by monitoring in the tracking stage can be evaluated and corrected. For example, you can see whether a delay is significant and thus likely to affect the critical path or whether it is relatively unimportant.

● **reporting changes**

You need both to record changes to the work breakdown structure or similar project initiation document by updating the project status and also to inform the key stakeholders of significant changes in the project, for example at regular progress meetings.

We now look at implementing these processes.

Dealing with risks

On Monday, we defined risks as uncertain events that could affect the successful implementation of a project. Your aim should be to identify such risks before they occur and do all you can to reduce the likelihood of their occurrence and minimize their effects.

You will not survive a project without encountering certain risks, so it is better to plan to deal with them rather than be surprised when they unexpectedly arise.

On Monday, we identified the need in the planning stage to prepare a risk-assessment document. This document should list potential risks, their probability of occurrence, the extent of their effect on your project objectives and your responses to them.

It is important to consider possible risks by identifying the situations that could result in risks. For example, a company might launch a new technology product that is a smartphone or an ereader. Since technology is changing fast in these areas significant changes in the marketplace are likely, leading to changes in demand and consequently potentially to significant lower returns on investment.

It is important to record risks and the action taken to resolve them. You should review risks regularly.

A record of risks is called a **risk log** or a **risk register**. Typically, such a record consists of:

- risk ID number: a unique number to identify the risk
- identifier: the colleague who raised the risk
- date: the date on which the risk was first identified
- description: a brief but clear description of the risk
- probability: the likelihood of the risk's occurrence – low, medium or high
- effect: the impact of the risk on the project – low, medium or high
- response: measures taken to counteract the risk
- owner: the colleague assigned to deal with the risk
- status: whether the risk has been dealt with or not.

Risks may develop into issues – significant matters that will jeopardize the completion of the project. Again, such matters should be identified, logged and assessed, and actions planned and agreed. To deal with these, you may need to identify and have authorized additional resources. You will then need to monitor the measures taken, to ensure that they are effective.

Example of risk assessment for a holiday booking company

ID	Identifier	Date	Description	Probability	Effect	Response	Owner	Status
001	HLN	01/03/16	Inadequate publicity	Low	Medium	Revise publicity	NJS	Going to new supplier
002	HLN	15/03/16	Computer software breakdown	Medium	High	Ensure technicians are available 24/7	NJS	Tech guys on standby
003	BRJ	20/03/16	Too many bookings	Medium	High	Identify other accommodation	SJC	Hotels provisionally booked
004	BRJ	25/03/16	Poor weather	Medium	High	Include holidays with indoor activities	SJC	Indoor activities planned

Case study: Unclear roles

A publishing company outsourced the compilation of a new medical reference text to Harry as Managing Editor. Together with the sponsoring director at the publishers, Harry gathered a team of consultants, compilers and editors. Only once the project was under way did it become apparent that, although he was good at organizing, Harry lacked sufficient specialist medical knowledge to brief the editors and compilers fully. The result was that the project was put on hold for several months while a general editor with excellent knowledge of the medical field was found to work alongside Harry. Funds were agreed to finance such a role. The end result of clarified roles was an excellent reference tool.

Control your costs

To ensure control of your costs, you need to:

● **keep to the agreed budget**
If additional expenditure is needed, you should have allowed for it that in your contingency funds. If not, you will need to present a good case to senior management for extra funding.

● **make sure that all expenditure is carefully recorded**
This includes costs of staff and equipment (e.g. computers, offices) – that all expenditure is regularly assigned to cost centres and that you monitor such expenditure regularly. Normally, expenditure is tracked monthly, with progress reports being given at three-monthly intervals.

● **make sure that any income is also carefully recorded**

● **prepare monthly summary statements** that include:
 – the overall actual expenditure and income incurred up to a particular point, set alongside the total project budget
 – the costs incurred in the period under review
 – the costs incurred since the beginning of the project
 – the percentage of the work completed.

Example of a monthly statement for a project to plan a conference

	February 2016		
Item	Actual expenditure	Monthly budgeted expenditure[1]	Notes
Speaker: fee on agreement	1,500	1,000	2
Venue deposit	2,000	800	3
Publicity	1,000	400	4
Salaries	20,000	20,000	5
Office equipment	3,000	1,800	6
Other overheads	1,000	1,000	
Total costs in February	28,500	25,000	
Contingency: one month		2,500	
Total costs in February including contingency	28,500	27,500	7
Contingency in overall budget		15,000	
Overall budget		**£165,000**	

Costs incurred so far in project: £28,500; % of work completed: 16.7%.
Income: 0 [due to receive bookings from 1 March onwards]

Notes

1 The monthly budgeted figures show the total for the whole project (£165,000) divided by the number of months (6), i.e. £165,000 divided by 6 = £27,500.
2 The speaker's costs are £6,000. This figure divided by six (for each of six months) = £1,000. But she was paid £1,500 in February on agreement to speak, with the rest being paid at the end of the conference.
3 The overall cost of the venue is £4,800. This figure divided by six (for each of six months) is £800. The conference centre asked for a £2,000 deposit, which was paid in February.
4 The overall cost of publicity is £2,400. This figure divided by six = £400. In February, £1,000 was spent: obviously the advertising needs to go out well in advance of the conference and so costs in the initial months are higher than later in the project.
5 Actual salaries are in line with projected salaries.
6 Office equipment. The £1,800 is an average monthly figure, with a budget total of £1,800 divided by six = £8,400; new computer systems were bought at the beginning of the project – hence the greater amount.
7 The conclusion is that, although expenditure in February 2016 exceeded the amount allowed for, even including contingency, by £1,000 (£28,500 – £27,500), overall the project is on track financially because higher initial costs were incurred which will not be repeated later.

Monitoring all expenditure

It's important to monitor *all* expenditure, including the costs of all the colleagues who are working on the project. All staff need to fill in time sheets regularly so that you can track and monitor the expenditure. Make sure that you have accurate figures on hourly rates, according to the system you have chosen to adopt, including or excluding general business overheads (see Tuesday).

Plan for change

Since there are likely to be changes during the lifetime of your project, you will need to take steps to minimize their effect. Ways in which you can minimize the effects of change include:

● **preparing a disaster recovery plan**
A disaster recovery plan is a document your company or organization should have in place in case of a major incident such as extreme weather, a fire at your offices or a major terrorist alert. This should list contact details of staff, insurers, major suppliers and procedures to be followed. For example, if there is a severe weather warning, a prolonged transport strike or a major terrorist alert, staff should be able to work from home with remote access to their computers. By having procedures – such as for backing up computer files – in place *before* an incident occurs, you can minimize the effects of disruption.

● **recording roles and responsibilities**
If a key member of your project team unexpectedly resigns or suffers a major illness, then you will at least be aware of that colleague's responsibilities and can adjust team members accordingly.

● **dealing with internal changes to the project**
For example, you may encounter technical problems or your customer may change his or her mind (for example, while you are redesigning their website they may now think it would be a good idea if you could also help them improve their online ordering system at the same time). In such instances, base your decision about whether to make the change on the following information:

- the source of the request for change
- the reasons for such a request
- the effects of (a) making such a change, for example on schedules, products and resources, and (b) the effects of not making such a change
- the cost of making such a change.

Deciding to make a change

If you do decide to make a change:
● note in writing the steps you are taking to bring about the change
● update your project plan (amend your work breakdown structure and product implementation document), for example in terms of schedules
● update your budget
● communicate the change to the relevant colleagues and stakeholders.

Scope creep

The term **scope creep** refers to a series of gradual small changes to a project that together have a significant effect on it. Examples of scope creep are:

● activities not included in your original plans, for example where colleagues have made what they consider minor changes without formal approval
● activities that take longer or cost more than originally planned.

You can control scope creep by:

- identifying the significant activities more effectively earlier in your planning
- assessing the effects of requested changes more thoroughly (see above)
- developing good relationships with your key colleagues so that your communications are better.

Case study: Unforeseen problems

An airline terminal had a project for routine maintenance of its conveyor-belt mechanisms to take passengers' suitcases from check-in areas to the correct aircraft.

A new conveyor-belt mechanism was fitted over a public holiday weekend, when passenger numbers were high. Unforeseen technical problems developed, however, which led to inconvenience and disruption and a few suitcases being misdirected. With hindsight, less disruption would have occurred if the routine maintenance had been planned for a period when the terminal was less busy.

Keep going!

There comes a time in a project, when you have all your systems in place and everything is going more or less smoothly, when you begin to wonder if the project will fail. At such a time, it is worth following these tips:

- Remain calm and determined. You have in place all your systems. Be confident that they represent effective work procedures.
- Stay focused. If problems do develop, be positive and focus on a solution rather than seeking to attach blame on an individual.
- Don't get so immersed in the details that you miss out on the big picture. See how far you have come as well as how far you still have to go.

- Think of the next step. As you consider that, reassess the planned time estimates and if necessary change them in advance, rather than discover too late that they were inaccurate.
- Look to your end product. I have worked on several multi-year large projects to produce major reference books. During the lengthy development periods of these projects, I imagine a picture of me holding the final product in my hands – this helps keep me going.
- Communicate well with others – both in your team and with your stakeholders (see also Thursday).
- Think creatively about ways you can work even more effectively. Be sensible. Are there even better ways to work?
- Deal with what is before you effectively. Remain positive, well motivated and committed. Do your best *now*.

IGNORE YOUR STAKEHOLDERS AT YOUR PERIL

Summary

Today we have been concerned with implementing the project and moving it forward. Once we have confirmed the key personnel involved and the available financial resources, we can establish the milestones in our project and set up systems that track and monitor progress, allowing us to track, control and report any changes. We learned the importance of dealing with risks proactively, and of tracking and monitoring actual expenditure against the project budget.

We also learned how to plan for changes, large and small, and about the importance of keeping going, even in the face of difficulties, with tips for remaining positive and determined.

Now take the following practical steps:

1 As the project begins, confirm commitments of all your key colleagues.

2 Throughout the development of the project, keep the budget and cash flow as accurate as possible.

3 Throughout the development of the project, keep your work breakdown structure (WBS) / project initiation document (PID) as accurate and up to date as possible.

4 Make sure that you have effective control procedures that regularly monitor and report changes, especially in costs and schedules.

5 Start and maintain a risk log.

6 Prepare a disaster recovery plan.

Fact-check [answers at the back]

1. What are project milestones?
   a) The foundation stones of your office building ❏
   b) The problems that loom large in your mind ❏
   c) The key costs of your project ❏
   d) The key dates and events in a project ❏

2. What does PID stand for?
   a) Project injection document ❏
   b) Plan invention document ❏
   c) Project initiation document ❏
   d) Project initiation and development ❏

3. What does tracking changes involve?
   a) Monitoring and reporting changes to control them ❏
   b) Monitoring and reporting changes to increase them ❏
   c) Reporting only positive changes to the project board ❏
   d) Only monitoring changes and doing nothing with your results ❏

4. What is a risk log?
   a) A chocolate log ❏
   b) A thick branch ❏
   c) A record of the changes to the project's costs ❏
   d) A record of risks to the project ❏

5. What should a disaster recovery plan cover?
   a) A change in your project costs ❏
   b) A plan if you have a cold ❏
   c) A fire in the suburbs, 10 kilometres from your office ❏
   d) A fire at your office ❏

6. What is 'scope creep'?
   a) A sycophantic colleague ❏
   b) The major changes to a project that you have recognized ❏
   c) The series of small changes to a project that can have a significant effect on it ❏
   d) The series of small changes to a project that can have an insignificant effect on it ❏

7. What should you do if a project starts to go wrong?
   a) Phone your boss ❏
   b) Look at your notes ❏
   c) Find a solution first ❏
   d) Focus on blaming someone ❏

8. As you carry out the project, what should you focus on?
   a) Your project team ❏
   b) Your procedures ❏
   c) The start ❏
   d) The end result and customers ❏

9. As you implement the project, what should you focus on?
   a) Remaining static and not changing anything ❏
   b) Being creative and thinking up unusual ways to solve easy problems ❏
   c) Being flexible in solving problems ❏
   d) Panicking over every problem ❏

10. In project management, what should you never do?
    a) Focus on the big picture ❏
    b) Lose sight of your goal ❏
    c) Do your best now ❏
    d) Think about the next step ❏

THURSDAY

Communicate effectively

You have now completed all your preparation and planning. Your project has been costed as accurately as you think possible and you are putting it into practice. How do you do this? You *communicate* with others: with your team, your project sponsor and your key stakeholders.

This may sound easy, but failures to communicate well are a significant reason why projects fail. Roles and responsibilities cross over and you spend a lot of time sorting out who should be doing what, when it would have been better if all that had been clarified earlier. When colleagues are not kept informed, and the cry goes up, 'You've not told us anything about this – it's the first we've heard about it,' this is the moment when you realize that communication should have been better planned and carried out.

Today we will stand back and consider the different ways in which you should communicate in a project, through listening, delegating, use of email, telephone, meetings, progress reports, effective leadership, good teamwork, resolving conflict and negotiating.

Listening

Listening may seem a strange place to start, but as is often stated, 'God gave us two ears and one mouth,' so before we are tempted to speak it is wise to listen.

You need to listen at every stage of the project:

1 In the **preparatory stage** of thinking, you need to listen to your customers' or users' needs so that the contents of your project match their requirements.
2 In the **planning and costing stages** as you continue to lay a strong foundation, check that the colleagues you work with understand you and one another.
3 In the **implementation stage,** you need to listen to your customers or users in case they want changes to the project, and to colleagues as they work out their roles. Are they struggling to understand the brief you have given them? Shouting more loudly at them won't help – you need to listen.

Some effects of listening

Listening:

● focuses on the other person. Often when someone else is talking, we are focusing on thinking about what we are going to say as a reply. Stop and really listen to what the other person is saying. Make eye contact with them. Rephrase what they have said in your own way to help you clarify the meaning in your own mind (for example, 'So what you're really saying is that the whole process needs to be looked at again'); this process is called 'reflective listening'

- values the person you are listening to as an individual in their own right, so that you understand 'where they're coming from', why they are working or speaking as they are
- means that you do not listen only to the words a colleague is speaking: you can perceive their response to what you are saying by being sensitive to their body language and tone of voice
- allows you to 'listen between the lines', to become aware of any underlying messages – your response could be, for example, 'So I guess what you're saying is that you need someone else to help you complete this task on time'
- builds trust between people: you show that you are genuinely interested in them. This forms the basis to help you work well with them.

Case study: Susie was angry

Susie was angry. She worked late every evening to complete her tasks in the project but she felt her work was not appreciated or valued. It was only when a new colleague, Jan, started to work alongside her that something happened. Jan was not concerned only about herself and her own work (which she did well), but also cared enough about her colleague to stop and listen to her. Susie was in tears as she poured out her heart to Jan, and at the end of their conversation Susie told Jan, 'Thanks for listening. You're the first person I've been able to talk to about these things.'

The basics of communication

In the seminars I lead, I discuss the basics of communication under the headings A I R:

- **Audience:** we adapt what to communicate according to our audience, so, for example, an email to a colleague at the next desk to us will be written in a different tone from one to the company's managing director
- **Intention:** what exactly are you trying to communicate? What is your message? If you are not clear about it, the readers of your email won't be clear either. On one of my courses, a participant's key message was buried in brackets at the end of a 67-word sentence!
- **Response:** what are you expecting your colleague to do as a result of your communication with him or her? Have you made clear what you want your colleague to do next? You don't want them to say, 'Yes, I get that, but so what?'

A communications plan

It can be helpful to draw up a communications plan. This lists:

- the **person or group** you need to communicate with
- the kind of **information** you need to communicate
- the **purpose** of the communication: for example, reporting progress, finding solutions to problems
- the **method** you will use to communicate the information: for example, email, meetings, reports, phone calls
- the **frequency** with which you will communicate the information.

Delegating work

In briefing or in delegating others, you need to:

- choose colleagues who are experienced and skilled enough to take on the task; otherwise you will need to provide training for them
- be clear about the task or activity that you want your colleague to undertake
- where possible, follow up any spoken instructions in writing with a full brief, outlining the work
- break the task or activity down into its parts. Write briefing instructions, but don't just write in abstract terms; give examples of what needs to be done

- give background details, so that the colleague knows where their task or activity fits into the overall scheme of things, without, however, giving an exhaustive account of all the details
- provide an opportunity for your colleague to ask questions to clarify what you want them to do
- state the date and time by which you want your colleague to complete the work
- supervise their work properly: provide the equipment and other resources that the colleague needs. Discuss any difficulties that arise, together with possible solutions. Monitor their progress during the project and evaluate it at the end of the project.

Email

Emails are great: we can communicate with colleagues all round the world instantly. But emails also have their disadvantages. We can receive too many unwanted ones that stop us dealing with the tasks we are supposed to be dealing with.

Here are a few tips:

- Put a clear subject in the subject line: this will help your reader know what the email is about.
- Use 'cc' ('carbon copy', from the days of paper) and 'bcc' ('blind carbon copy') sparingly. Only send copies to those who really need to see the email.

 What are cc and bcc?
If I am emailing Colin and cc Derek and bcc Ed, then Colin will see I have copied the email to Derek but Colin will not see I have copied the email to Ed. ('bcc' can also be useful for bulk emails when you don't want individuals to know the identity of the people on your emailing list.)

- Unless you are writing to a close colleague, include some form of opening and closing greetings. The policy of your company and organization and your own personality will guide you to what is acceptable (for example, I find 'Hi Martin' difficult to accept from someone I don't know at all).

- In a long email, put the key information at the beginning, so that it will be clear on the opening screenshot as your reader opens the email.
- Use abbreviations that are generally known, not obscure ones.
- Don't use capitals, which indicate shouting.
- Include other contact information at the end of your email (including your job title, phone numbers (landline, mobile) and postal address). Your reader might just want to phone you to clarify a point.

As with all forms of communication, check that what you are saying is accurate before you send it. We've all received emails inviting us to a meeting on Tuesday 14 September, only to discover that 14 September is a Wednesday. The result is that many colleagues spend precious time emailing requests for clarification, and then time has to be spent responding to them with the exact date. It would have been better if the person who originally sent the message had checked the details before sending it.

Reading emails

Try to discipline yourself to opening and responding to emails at just a few points during the day, rather than having it on all the time. In periods that require concentrated work, switch your emails off. The time taken to open an email and then 'I'll just reply to this now I've opened it' adds up and can have a significant effect on your overall work.

Choose the right medium

Email is not always the right medium for your message; we have all heard of colleagues being dismissed by email (or text message), so do consider whether email is appropriate. Messages about sensitive matters are best dealt with face to face, and followed up in writing. An email serves well to clarify a quick point, or to announce the date of a meeting and its agenda. Don't neglect the old-fashioned phone, though: that remains a useful tool to build and develop professional relationships.

Meetings

Sometimes it seems as if life consists of going from one meeting to another, without actually achieving anything. How can we make sure the meetings we attend count? We can consider:

- the purpose of meetings
- preparing for meetings
- chairing meetings
- participating in meetings
- following up from meetings.

The purpose of meetings

Meetings are useful to:

- give colleagues **information**, for example about a new proposal or progress
- discuss **issues** with colleagues, for example about negotiations on the terms of a contract, the way ahead or a solution to a problem
- reach a **decision** and agree on the next steps to be taken.

Preparing for meetings

The key to a successful meeting lies in the preparation. It is essential that you prepare in the following ways:

- **Know the purpose of the meeting**. Many of our meetings have no clear purpose and could easily be shortened or even cancelled. You need to be crystal clear about what you are trying to achieve.
- **Plan a venue and time** (start, finish) in advance. I have been to meetings at the stated venue but arrived there to find that the meeting is in a different place.
- **Invite the key people** to participate well in advance. If you want a boss with a busy diary to be present, it is no good inviting him or her the day before; you need to have invited them a long time before. It is also useful if you can discuss with key people in advance any agenda items that could be controversial.

- **Circulate an agenda in advance**. This means that you will have thought about the structure and purpose of the meeting beforehand. Also, circulate important papers with the agenda, not at the meeting itself. Ideally, the length of such papers should be no more than one page
- **Prepare the meeting room**. Plan the seating: chairs around a table invite discussion; a chairperson at the end of a long table with ten seats on either side, less so. If a PowerPoint presentation is being given, ensure that you have a projector and connecting lead set up. Check that the heating or air conditioning works.
- **Read reports in advance**. If reports have been circulated before a meeting, read them. I have been in too many meetings where we have sat during the meeting reading material, something that should have been undertaken in advance.
- **Ensure that you come up with accurate information**. If the meeting is one to monitor progress, take all your latest data on progress with you.

Chairing meetings

The chairperson – or chair – is the one who sets the tone for the meeting and guides the participants through the discussion. His or her tasks include:

- keeping to the agenda so that the meeting finishes on time
- bringing in key individuals to contribute at appropriate points
- summarizing progress
- drawing together the points discussed, to reach conclusions and to make decisions (if a point has been controversial, the chair can express exactly what is to be minuted, to avoid possible misinterpretation later)
- ensuring that action points are clear, particularly for those responsible for following up particular points. The action points should be SMART: specific, measurable, agreed, realistic and timed (see also Sunday).

A good chair is a diplomatic and organized leader, someone whom the colleagues trust, who values, motivates and involves others. Ideally, he or she will be able to quieten those who talk too much and draw out those who talk too little. He or she will sense when the time is right to bring a discussion to an end and be able to come to clear decisions.

Participating in meetings

> *'Any committee is only as good as the most knowledgeable, determined and vigorous person on it. There must be somebody who provides the flame.'*
>
> Claudia ('Lady Bird') Johnson (1912–2007), widow of US President Lyndon B. Johnson

Everyone has a part to play in a successful meeting. I have never understood how people can come out of a meeting asking, 'What was the point of that?' when they themselves have not contributed anything. Each of us has a role to play, by:

- **listening well and concentrating:** switch off your phone; avoid sending text messages
- **asking for clarification:** if we are unsure about a point that has been made, it is highly likely that other colleagues are too, but have been afraid to ask for fear of looking ignorant
- **being constructive:** even if we disagree with what has been said there are positive ways of expressing a difference of opinion without angry criticism of the other person
- **confronting issues:** focus on the real issues; too many meetings avoid discussing 'the elephant in the room', the subject everyone is aware of but which is not discussed because it is too uncomfortable – don't get sidetracked!
- **being willing to change your mind:** if you are listening and persuasive arguments have been offered, allow yourself to be convinced by them and change your opinion about an issue.

Following up from meetings

A meeting is a waste of time if decisions were made but no one acts on these decisions. If colleagues have action points to pursue, they should follow them up.

The **minutes** of a meeting are a record of what happened during the meeting, especially its action points. The person taking the minutes does not need to write down everything that goes on, but must note specifically the significant decisions, especially those concerning dates, schedules and financial matters.

The sooner the minutes of a meeting are circulated to those present at the meeting and other key colleagues, the more likely it is that colleagues will follow up the action points asked of them.

A good project leader will also follow through on progress of the key action items; he or she will not leave it to the next meeting, only to discover that action has not been taken and valuable time has been lost.

Case study: Rescuing a failing project

Imran was called in to troubleshoot on a failing project, where the existing project manager was beginning not to cope with the growing responsibilities of the project. Fortunately, Imran had a good working relationship with him.

Imran quickly noticed that basic points were missing: meetings were poorly structured with the barest agenda. During the meetings, discussions rambled on for a long time, often without decisions being made. Even when key action points were agreed, they were not noted, followed through or ever reviewed at further meetings. No wonder the project was in a mess! As Imran had good relationships with all the colleagues, he was quickly able to put in place well-structured meetings with good chairmanship, minute taking, action points and reviews at the following meeting. In this way the project got back on track.

Progress reports

As project manager you will need to update your steering committee or project board and other colleagues regularly. Your reports should:

- be presented in a standard format every time, not one that varies. Consider using different colours to indicate various aspects of your report, for example the different stages
- contain a summary of the project's overall progress
- contain all the significant facts relating to a stated time period; for example:
  - actual work undertaken, the stages completed, output produced
  - actual time spent on the stages, usually in hours
  - actual costs incurred
  - actual expenditure made
- particular achievements, such as milestones or other targets reached
- variations from expected figures in terms of work (output, products), timings, costs and payment
- reasons for variations from original or approved estimates, for example explanations of delay or excessive expenditure
- other issues (including any risks from your risk-management procedures), including, where possible, statements of the actions to be taken to resolve them
- a forecast of the new final projected date and costs, on the basis of the information in your progress report
- a note of changes approved
- a plan of the significant outputs and achievements that you are planning for the following reporting period, together with a note of possible difficulties you expect to encounter and how you will resolve them.

Put it in writing

As with any other form of communication:

- think about your audience, intention and response (see 'The basics of communication', above). This will determine, for example, how much information you should include in your reports. If in doubt, discuss with colleagues
- make sure your message is well planned and well structured
- write clearly and, if possible, simply, using only those abbreviations and technical expressions that the readers of your report are familiar with

be as concise as possible. You may have heard of the quotation, 'I have written you a long letter because I didn't have time to write you a short one.' Writing concisely is an art to be learned – but it is very useful. If the report is long, present a one-page summary at the beginning

- use correct grammar and proper punctuation. Shortage of time is no excuse for using careless or sloppy English or the forms of abbreviation (textspeak, SMS language) you use to close friends.

Teamwork

We are used to thinking of teams in the contexts of sports. The project manager is the leader of a team, and as such is responsible for certain actions, as follows.

- Choose the personnel, especially the key colleagues, carefully. Choose colleagues who are skilled and experienced or those who can develop well with training. Having inexperienced staff on the team will affect the whole team and mean that you have to spend undue amounts of time helping them.
- Be clear about the goals. Keep your team members informed, about the bad news as well as the good. Plan your persuasive arguments well. Present them strongly, with inspiration and realism.
- Work out the different roles and responsibilities of team members, according to their skills and abilities. Using the Belbin approach to team role analysis is a useful way to think about this. (At an awayday for a group I am connected with I ended up (re-)discovering my chairing skills, so I was formally asked to chair meetings.)
- Set a consistent example. For example, your colleagues will lose motivation if you ask them to work extra hours when you often leave promptly or early. Model the qualities – being available, listening well – that you are trying to encourage in others. Practise what you preach.
- Respect others: appreciate their contributions, recognize individual team members' achievements publicly. Keep working on your professional relationships to develop trust.

- Set targets that make the teamwork hard but that are not totally unrealistic (colleagues recently asked me to undertake 87 days' work in 10 days!).

- Be flexible about what is negotiable and about different styles of working. Be prepared to 'think outside the box' creatively to challenge existing patterns of thinking and working and find solutions to difficulties.
- Stay focused and determined to complete the task. (Colleagues have been impressed that I have completed three multi-year projects – each five to seven years in duration – and feel inclined to trust me with similar projects in the future.)
- Deal with conflict quickly, tackling the issues: don't be too cautious and fearful about speaking directly and clearly about difficulties. There is no need to do this all the time, however: you need to balance out this quality with ones that show empathy.
- Be fair and treat all your colleagues equally, even though you may like some more than others.

Reward your team in an appropriate way, for example by taking them all out (with partners) for a celebration meal at the end of the project.

Resolving conflict

The authors of the books *Difficult Conversations: How to Discuss What Matters Most* by Douglas Stone, Bruce Patton and Sheila Heen (Michael Joseph, 1999) and *The Peacemaker: A Biblical Guide to Resolving Personal Conflict* by Ken Sande (Baker, 1991) helpfully suggest how you can resolve conflict, as follows:

1 Distinguish the incident – what happened – from feelings about the incident. Consider separately:
   - the incident – someone said something; someone is to blame. Try to focus on the real issue, and understand other people's interests as well as your own
   - feelings about the incident, such as anger or hurt
   - the identity of the other people involved, including their self-worth, which may feel threatened; calmly affirm your respect for them.
2 Do what you can to resolve the issue and maintain the relationship if possible: prepare and evaluate possible solutions.

Case study: The four stages of building a team

A project team was appointed to develop a change-management strategy (see also Friday). When the team first met, everyone was friendly and there was a sense of excitement as the project leader explained the project's aims and they began to work out their roles (**'forming'**). Fairly quickly, however, issues began to surface as different colleagues had different perspectives and conflicts began to emerge (**'storming'**).

Gradually, the team members worked through these challenges and, although discussions still became heated at times, they began to trust one another and were able to reach broad agreement on the way ahead (**'norming'**). They were then able to work well together to formulate and eventually implement the strategy (**'performing'**). (The names of the stages were devised by the US psychologist Bruce Tuckman.)

Negotiate: win-win situations

In negotiating, we are aiming for a win-win situation. (This is different from behaviour where one person wins at the expense of another's loss.) A win-win situation can perhaps be well illustrated by an example. My son Ben has just moved to Asia and he wanted to sell his camera. His friend Rob wanted a camera to take photographs on his travels. Ben sold Rob his camera, so both won: both gained what they wanted: Ben money, Rob a camera.

In his book *Seven Habits of Highly Effective People*, Stephen Covey points out that the basics of a win-win situation is our character:

'If you're high on courage and low on consideration, how will you think? Win-Lose. You'll be strong and ego-bound. You'll have the courage of your convictions, but you won't be very considerate of others... If you're high on consideration and low on courage, you'll think Lose-Win. You'll be so considerate of others' feelings that you won't have the courage to express your own... High courage and consideration are both essential to

Win-Win. It's the balance of the two that is the mark of real maturity. If you have it, you can listen and you can empathically understand, but you can also courageously confront.'

Steven Covey,*Seven Habits of Highly Effective People Personal Handbook* (Simon & Schuster, 2003), page 91

Case study: A good negotiator

Danielle was respected as a good negotiator in contracts. The secret of her success lay in good planning. She spent a long time thinking through different business models and pricing levels so that, when it came to the negotiations, she knew exactly what approach to take.

After both sides had presented their initial case, she was sometimes able to detect the weak points in the arguments of the other side and exploit them according to her own personality. When they came to the final bargaining she knew which of the less significant matters she could be flexible on but was firm on what was non-negotiable. She was not cautious about closing the deal and arranging the next steps in business relationships between the two sides.

Summary

Today has been concerned with learning about the skills we need in order to communicate more effectively. These skills include knowing how to listen well and understanding whom we are communicating with, what we want to communicate and what response we expect. Good communication skills allow us to delegate successfully, use different media such as phone and email effectively, run better meetings and writing good progress reports. We also looked at how better communications allow teams to function well, and how learning ways to resolve conflict and develop negotiating skills allows us to become a more effective team leader.

Now consider what practical steps you need to take to improve:

1 your listening skills

2 your planning of the purpose of an email, a meeting or negotiations

3 your ability to delegate

4 the effectiveness of your meetings

5 your leadership skills

6 your ability to resolve conflict

7 your negotiation skills.

SUNDAY
MONDAY
TUESDAY
WEDNESDAY
THURSDAY
FRIDAY
SATURDAY

Fact-check [answers at the back]

1. What is reflective listening?
a) Thinking about listening ❏
b) Rephrasing what someone has said to you ❏
c) Listening to yourself while looking in a mirror ❏
d) Meditating on the meaning of life ❏

2. What does a communications plan need to list?
a) Only the people you need to communicate with ❏
b) Only the information you need to communicate ❏
c) Colleagues' email, phone and office contact details ❏
d) The information you need to communicate and the people you need to communicate it to ❏

3. What should you do when delegating work?
a) Write a clear, concise brief that excludes possible difficulties ❏
b) Write a clear, concise brief that includes possible difficulties ❏
c) Hope that colleagues will pick up what you want ❏
d) Don't bother to write a brief ❏

4. When sending emails, when should you use the cc function?
a) To everyone who could possibly have an interest in the subject ❏
b) Sparingly, only to those who really need to see the email ❏
c) All the time ❏
d) I don't know what cc stands for ❏

5. When should you read and answer emails?
a) As soon as they arrive, including those not related to work ❏
b) Every Friday afternoon ❏
c) At particular times, so that you can concentrate on your work ❏
d) Never answer them at all ❏

6. What should you do when attending a meeting?
a) Arrive late ❏
b) Fiddle with a pen ❏
c) Arrive promptly, having read the agenda and reports ❏
d) Arrive promptly, not having read the agenda and reports ❏

7. During meetings, what should you do?
a) Be indecisive ❏
b) Never reach a decision ❏
c) Come to decisions but not bother to record them ❏
d) Come to decisions and ensure that they are properly recorded and reviewed ❏

8. Ideally, what should a team consist of?
a) People with different skills and abilities ❏
b) People with the same skills and abilities ❏
c) People with different personalities ❏
d) People with the same personalities ❏

9. What's the best way to resolve conflict?
a) Ignore people's feelings ❑
b) Go straight into fixing it, without listening to what happened ❑
c) Only listen to people's feelings and ignore the real issues ❑
d) Distinguish the issue from colleagues' emotional responses to the issue ❑

10. What should be your aim when negotiating?
a) To win at all costs ❑
b) To have a win-win situation on both sides ❑
c) To settle the discussion as quickly as possible ❑
d) To show off how good you are ❑

FRIDAY

Deal with change constructively

Why do some projects go wrong? What are the main reasons for failure? You may think you have done your best, but still your project loses its way, gets stuck, loses momentum and grinds to a halt. You feel you are making no progress at all.

Today we look at some of the common reasons for failure... but we want to be constructive too, because no project is so hopeless that it cannot be redeemed and put back on track. We will consider measures you can take to look at why your project is failing and what you can do to retrieve it. We will focus again on the core issues of your objectives, personnel, activities, quality, costs and schedules. We will also look at how you can put in place better procedures to monitor and control your project's activities, quality, costs and schedules.

Ultimately, all project management is concerned with changes, so today we will also look at how you, as project manager, can manage those changes You will learn techniques for dealing with people who are resistant to change and how to lead and manage changes effectively.

Problems that may arise

The main problems that may arise during your management of a project often occur because of poor set-up or implementation.

Problems with poor set-up

If your project was not thought through carefully enough at the outset, problems can arise. These problems may be due to such things as:

- aims that were defined only vaguely, not precisely (look back at Sunday and Monday)
- weak support and commitment from senior management. If senior managers are half-hearted or unenthusiastic about the project, their lack of influence will be contagious (see Sunday and Monday)
- lack of ownership by stakeholders. Unless the stakeholders are committed to the project, it will fail (see Sunday and Monday)
- inadequate experience and skills on the part of team members. You thought that colleagues' knowledge and abilities were far greater than they proved to be (see Monday)
- poorly defined roles and responsibilities, resulting in confusion. No one knows who is supposed to do what (see Monday and Thursday)

- insufficient resources (especially financial) allocated to the project (see Tuesday). The resources needed were significantly underestimated
- unrealistic estimates in the original plan
- weak leadership (look at Thursday).

Problems with poor implementation

It may be that the project was thought through fairly carefully at the initial stage, but has failed at the implementation stage (see also Wednesday). The following problems may then arise.

- Team members are not available at the correct times to undertake the work.
- The schedule slips because inadequate or ineffective monitoring and control procedures are in place.
- Unforeseen technical problems arise during the course of the project.
- Unexpected risks occur that have a significant effect on costs and schedules.
- Bad communications, poor relationships and a lack of teamwork (see also Thursday) are significant.
- Significant changes occur during the project that cause it to fail.
- The end users do not fully accept the project's outcomes.

SUNDAY
MONDAY
TUESDAY
WEDNESDAY
THURSDAY
FRIDAY
SATURDAY

Case study: Edinburgh's tram system

Plans for a tram network in Edinburgh began in 2000. The hope was that by 2008 there would be a network of at least three lines, but months after the works started costs started to get out of control. Digging work revealed unrecorded utility pipes. Following many setbacks, including cost overruns, delays and disagreements, the project (for a shorter route than originally planned) was eventually back on track and operation began in 2014.

Getting your project running again

If your project has lost momentum or has seriously been derailed, all is not lost. To get it back on track, you need to focus again on:

● **the project's purposes**
Record your goals and aims. Look at your users and your original outcomes. If necessary, modify them. Make sure that your new aims are SMART (see Sunday).

Case study: A facilitation meeting

The project team had got stuck. They had listed all their aims and discussed various strategies. They called a meeting of the key stakeholders to facilitate the next steps, and had an open discussion on the best way forward. The project manager and bosses were quiet and were surprised at the way middle managers picked up the vision and made concrete suggestions for the next steps. Having an open discussion with key colleagues not only helped to point the way forward but also showed who future leaders could be.

the project's personnel

Look again at the project team and make sure the roles
and responsibilities are clear. Deal with any relationship
issues that may have emerged. Obtain the specific, focused
commitment of every member of the team to complete the
project. Do you need additional personnel to complete all the
tasks on time? If so, cost them in, gain approval and ensure
that they are assigned to the project as soon as possible.

In particular, make the key personnel in the project more
accountable by:

- obtaining the agreement of a colleague's supervisor
  so that the colleague can work on the project for the
  specified duration
- clarifying carefully the work that needs to be done.
  (I recently delegated some work to a colleague and
  thankfully had allowed myself quality time to write a
  briefing document, which took me two hours to prepare.
  But because I was specific on the tasks, outcomes, time
  required and date by when I wanted the work completed,
  delegation of the work was effective.)
- gaining colleagues' agreement on the monitoring of their
  work. (This isn't 'checking up on someone' as if you don't
  trust them; this is part of the project. Done properly, it
  shows that you value that person and their work; it may
  also help you recognize warning signs if difficulties do
  arise as well as providing an opportunity for colleagues to
  ask you questions.)
- valuing colleagues' work when it is well done and affirming
  them in front of other people. Such tokens of appreciation
  (even a simple 'Thank you') are important.

the project's stages

Redefine what needs to happen at each stage. Record the
activities that still need to be undertaken. Add new activities;
confirm in writing, delete or alter the activities that are still
outstanding. For each activity, as accurately as you can,
record personnel, time and resources (especially financial)
required.

- **the project's schedule**
  Adjust your original schedule so that it now aligns with any revised projected date for the conclusion of the project. Set fresh milestones (key target dates) in the project.

- **the quality of what is delivered**
  Put in place measurable and objective criteria against which you can assess the quality of your outputs.

- **the project's risk management**
  If you have lapsed in logging (recording) risks (see Wednesday), re-engage in this. Identify, assess and deal with further possible unforeseen events so that their adverse effect on the project will be as small as possible.

- **the project's control systems**
  If the reason your project went off track was that you had inadequate monitoring and control procedures, you now need to make sure that you track actual activities against your revised plan and then effectively resolve any further issues that may arise.

Case study: Getting a project back on track

The plan for Smithshire Council to renovate the Doverville community centre had come to a halt. Residents didn't feel their views were valued; unforeseen severe weather in the winter had delayed the project beyond the planned spring opening; the council was running out of money.

The project manager, project sponsor, representatives of the Council and local residents – all the key stakeholders – held a meeting. Here, they focused on the way ahead rather than apportioning blame, and announced a revised plan to open in the autumn. Their renewed and focused commitment meant that the project was delivered to this revised timescale.

Change management

Another key aspect of project management is change management. Whether your project is large – such as restructuring a local authority to perform more effectively – or small – such as renovating a community centre – ultimately a key part of what you are doing is managing change. If progress on your project has slowed down significantly, for example, and you want to increase staff motivation, you will need to move your colleagues on from the 'We've always done it this way' way of thinking, which may be firmly embedded in their culture.

Responses to change

- **People don't like change**. 'We've always done it this way' is the mantra they may repeat. 'Things worked as they did – why do we need to change?'
- **People are uncomfortable with change**. Many people like routine and their patterns of life will undergo changes if changes are brought in.
- **People feel threatened by change**. Changes may affect a colleague's identity. If a shop-floor worker is promoted to management, he or she will have to work through issues of his or her personal identity because they are no longer 'one of the lads' (or 'lasses'), no longer part of 'us' but now 'them'.

Leading change

Here are some of the keys to leading change:

- **Understand your organization.**
  What is the organization's general atmosphere? Where are you? Is there a climate for change? Is the prevailing mood one of positive confidence, a 'can-do' supportive mentality, or are attitudes negative and cynical with a lot of backbiting and infighting? Be aware not only of what is going on at the centre of your organization but also at its edges and what is not (or no longer) going on. Talk to your colleagues and, even more importantly, listen to them (see also Thursday).

- **Emphasize the vision, the goal.**
  Don't get sidetracked with minor issues. Your company or organization's mission statement may be concerned with serving the community but that focus may have got lost. Refocus your key stakeholders' vision on that goal so that they understand it.

- **Emphasize the vision, the goal (again).**
  I have deliberately repeated this line from the previous paragraph because, again and again in managing change, you will constantly need to explain why you are doing what you are doing.

 TIP *In managing change, you will constantly need to explain why you are doing what you are doing.*

- **Convince colleagues that there must be change.**
  You will want commitment to change from senior management, the project team and your customers or end users, who will be affected by the changes. You need to explain clearly why changes are needed (for example because of falling productivity or decreasing profits as companies are choosing your competitors). You also need to show colleagues your destination, where you are aiming to lead them and the benefits changes will bring.

THEY SURVIVED THAT, NOW LET'S SEE IF THEY MANAGE THE JUMP!

- **Develop fresh values.**
  Turn your vision and goal into values that determine the emphasis and ethos of your company or organization. Make them as practical and simple as possible. (I led a writing course for a group of leading police officers and kept on asking them to simplify their values in ordinary words. It took two hours, at the end of which the boss said, 'Martin, you've changed my writing style in two hours!') You could perhaps develop the former values of your company or organization or you may need to rework them totally.

- **Develop a strategy.**
  As we have seen earlier this week, preparation and planning are essential, and so they are when we view project management from the approach of change management. It is vital to have a good strategy in place that will move you from your vision to your goal, through your values, to help earth your plans in reality.

- **Involve your colleagues.**
  In the early days of change management, involve the colleagues who will be part of the changes. Don't leave them 'out in the cold' or 'in the dark' till later: involve them in setting the vision and strategy and in making decisions.

- **Demonstrate committed leadership.**
  When you are trying to introduce change in an organization, it is vital that this is not seen as only one person's favourite subject. It is essential that the leader of such change gather

round him or her a group of other leaders who share that vision and a commitment to make it a reality. The senior leaders need these leaders to spend time with middle managers to make sure they catch the vision, so that the change can then be implemented throughout the organization.

● **Communicate well.**
As we saw on Thursday, good communication is essential in a project, and even more so when you want to move an organization through change. Rumours about possible changes to people's jobs, roles or location can all too easily arise and these can lower morale and lead to poor motivation. While formal public communications are significant, the informal, passing-in-the-corridor type conversations are also important. A boss who is always silent and remote and who only ever issues public announcements from his or her office will not foster good communications and trusting relationships in an organization. (One long-standing friend of mine deliberately allows extra time on a visit to the farthest end of his organization's workplace so that he can stop and talk to people on the way. Such informal communication – even a brief but genuine 'Good morning – how are you?' helps people feel valued for their contributions.)

TIP *Clear, well-thought-out, planned communications are vital, to bring your colleagues with you.*

● **Recognize achievements and efforts.**
Celebrate milestones. (One club I'm involved with in my spare time celebrated the initial decision to change with a meal for the committee in a restaurant.)

● **Stay focused on the goal, but be flexible on the way to reach the goal.**
Keep stating the goal and why there need to be changes but be willing to negotiate on the detail and style in which colleagues can reach the goal, so that they feel fully involved. Don't get sidetracked or deflected from pursuing your main goals by colleagues who want to make small unimportant changes.

● **Go for quick wins.**
Find an aspect of change that can be implemented fairly quickly and will produce the results you want, to demonstrate to the wider audience that change is happening and to bring about a positive response.

Case study: Key influencers

The project board for the renovation of the community centre opened up its meeting to a wider audience. The project manager and project sponsor were concerned about the response to their proposal to spend an additional £250,000 on adding a gym to the centre, to cater for the large number of young people who would be moving to the new housing estate that had just been approved by the Council. The project leaders feared that the wider audience of the meeting might reject the plan.

The whole tone of the meeting changed, however, when one senior, experienced and respected individual stood up at the beginning of the discussion and expressed his wholehearted and enthusiastic support for the proposal. After this contribution, the whole meeting then supported the proposal. Instead of rejecting it, they accepted it and recognized it as important. Having key influencers who can support your proposals for change is significant.

Summary

Today we learned how to discover why a project might be failing and how to bring it back on track by refocusing on the core issues of objectives, personnel, activities, the quality of outputs, costs and schedules. We looked at ways to ensure that better procedures are put in place to monitor and control activities and the quality of outputs, costs and schedules.

Today we have also been concerned with how we, as managers, can deal effectively with responses to change, and lead our company or organization successfully through times of change.

Now take the following practical steps:

1 Analyse why your project is behind schedule or has greater expenditure than planned.

2 Think what your three main priorities are to get your project back on track.

3 Communicate those priorities to your project co-workers.

4 Analyse why colleagues in your organization don't want to change.

5 Restate your aims as simply as possible.

6 Think of the steps you need to take to convince colleagues that there must be changes.

7 Think of a quick win.

SUNDAY
MONDAY
TUESDAY
WEDNESDAY
THURSDAY
FRIDAY
SATURDAY

Fact-check [answers at the back]

1. If a project is failing, what should you do?
   a) Nothing ❏
   b) Analyse why it is failing ❏
   c) Have a cup of tea ❏
   d) Redefine your aims vaguely ❏

2. Why do projects fail?
   a) Because schedules have been well managed ❏
   b) Because schedules have been poorly managed ❏
   c) Because schedules contain too much information ❏
   d) Because schedules contain too little information ❏

3. What is wholehearted commitment by senior management likely to lead to?
   a) My promotion ❏
   b) The project's failure ❏
   c) The project's success ❏
   d) A holiday ❏

4. What is refocusing on roles and responsibilities likely to lead to?
   a) The project's success ❏
   b) The project's failure ❏
   c) Confusion ❏
   d) Happiness ❏

5. To get a project back on track, what do you need to do?
   a) Blame the colleagues responsible for the delay ❏
   b) Replace all the staff ❏
   c) Take a holiday first ❏
   d) Go back to basics ❏

6. Should we show that we value our colleagues?
   a) No, it's someone else's job ❏
   b) Yes, it's essential ❏
   c) It's a 'nice-to-have' but not vital ❏
   d) It's a good thing if you have the time ❏

7. What is a typical response to change?
   a) Everyone likes change ❏
   b) Some people like change ❏
   c) I like change ❏
   d) Many people feel unhappy with change ❏

8. In a project to introduce change, what do you need to do?
   a) Be silent about why you are making the changes ❏
   b) Be silent once you are making the changes ❏
   c) Constantly state why you are making the changes ❏
   d) Criticize colleagues for their poor performance ❏

9. When leading an organization through change, how important are good communication and leadership?
   a) Unimportant ❏
   b) A luxury ❏
   c) A 'nice-to-have' ❏
   d) Essential ❏

10. What is a quick win?
   a) A part of the project that you hope will fail ❏
   b) A promotion ❏
   c) An aspect of change you can quickly implement and that will produce good results ❏
   d) A celebration of victory ❏

SATURDAY

Conclude and evaluate your project positively

Congratulations! You are nearly there in coming to grips with the basics of project management. You are drawing near the finishing line and completing your project. The day you thought would never come will soon be here. You can breathe a few sighs of relief... and what then?

Now is not the time to relax all the monitoring procedures that should have served you well during the running of the project. You need to keep them in place even as the project draws to a close, to maintain the momentum of the work right to the end.

Today we look at what you need to do to bring your project to a successful conclusion and to evaluate your experience of leading and running a project. You will discuss what went well and what could have gone better; you will then understand what lessons to learn and what mistakes to avoid next time, and what successes to note and celebrate.

Completing your project

As the project draws to completion, keep:

- tracking progress against your original plans
- monitoring and dealing with changes, especially to schedules and costs
- dealing with risks
- controlling your costs
- focused on your end goal: providing a quality product or service to your customers or users
- communicating well with all your colleagues.

You must now compile a list of the items you need to complete as clearly defined signs that the project has come to an end. You will have agreed these earlier in the project. They could include:

- ensuring the output of a certain number of products
- ensuring that the quality of what you deliver reaches the agreed criteria (for example verifying that a computer software system fulfils the required specifications) or undertaking other validating work according to agreed external criteria
- testing new equipment to make sure it all functions to the required standard
- training end users, for example, to use the equipment you have installed, or by preparing manuals or running courses
- identifying any other immediate project work that would be separate from, but associated with, your existing project that is coming to an end
- determining what, if any, support is needed after the project has come to an end
- completing final administrative tasks such as final progress reports, especially those concerned with financial resources.

Case study: Learning lessons

Last weekend I met Rodney, who has just retired from working for a council in northern England. In his final years at work he had gained a reputation for solving

Be aware of your team's emotions

As project leader, you should be aware of the motivations
and emotions of members of your team. Your colleagues are
probably tired and quite possibly stressed by the long, hard
work of the project. They may have had to work through a
series of changes during its lifetime, so treat them well! Their
levels of energy and enthusiasm may be beginning to go down,
so continue to:

- encourage them, constantly affirming the team's
  commitment to complete the project
- concentrate their attention on reaching the goal
- monitor and evaluate their work and your procedures to
  control schedules and costs
- remain available for colleagues to bring their concerns to you.

Final things

In every project I work on, I have a separate file called
'Final things'. I put in that file notes that I think may be
relevant in the final stages of a project, to bring the project
to a successful conclusion.

About two-thirds of the way through the project, I check
through this list to bring the project 'in to land', to use a
picture from a pilot flying a plane. I also look again at the
contract/scope of work and files of papers / computer files
that I have amassed during the project to make sure
I haven't missed anything significant.

Evaluating the completed project

The project is complete! You have celebrated and are basking in the glory of emails expressing congratulations. Is that it? Is there anything more to be done? Yes: you need to conduct post-project evaluation. This brings together the key points of the project so that you can see what went well, what did not go so well and also, significantly, what lessons you can learn for the future.

Some companies and organizations I have had experience of are so tightly controlled that it seems you are not allowed to be human. Others are at the opposite extreme and are so relaxed that you wonder how any work gets done or at least whether it runs at a profit or even covers costs. The ideal is surely somewhere in between, where colleagues are enabled to fulfil their potential but where procedures and guidelines are in place so that the company knows where it is going, especially as regards financial matters.

Acknowledge failures

In a company or organization with an open culture such as the one just described, mistakes are acceptable, for, as has been remarked, 'The person who never makes mistakes never made anything.' The critical thing here is to learn from your mistakes – neither to ignore them and pretend they did not happen or make them so widely known that blame is attached to an individual for the rest of his or her working life.

'The person who never makes mistakes never made anything.'

Anon.

If relationships are good (look back at Thursday), then trust and respect will have developed and the important thing – the completion of the project – will be uppermost. Don't be content with the superficial lesson. Look for the deeper reasons for, say, why a project was delayed:

- Were adequate monitoring controls in place?
- Were communications good between colleagues, or were key colleagues not informed about significant decisions?

However, you must ensure that the evaluation is professional: your purpose is not to attach blame to individuals but to be positive and to express a few certain realistic lessons that can be learned and applied in future projects. For example, don't say: 'Harry forgot to order the spare parts on time', but: 'Checks need to be made in advance that orders for spare parts are submitted two weeks before they are needed.' Any constructive criticism of an individual's contributions should be undertaken privately, not in a wider forum.

A good evaluation meeting

Recently I attended the evaluation meeting for the project to deliver 5,000 books that was mentioned on Tuesday. All the key colleagues who had taken part in the project were present. The decision to send 5,000 copies by air freight was applauded – the books were very well received and sold out at the exhibition. Minor suggestions were made to improve the design. Costs were reviewed and were slightly over budget. The response to the initial set was so good

Recognize success

As well as acknowledging failures, mistakes and where you could have undertaken the work better, it is also important to recognize those areas that have gone well, and **identify what you have achieved**. Specifically, list what you have delivered:

- solid planning and foundation on which the project was built
- strong support from your project sponsor
- the desired output in terms of the products, services, etc. that you have delivered
- outputs measured according to the agreed quality standards
- actual expenditure compared with the original budget (see below)
- a good return on investment: compare the benefits received from the project against the costs incurred
- the actual time taken compared with the original schedule; whether you delivered the outcomes on time or not
- the effective management of changes made throughout the project
- robust control procedures in place to track and monitor costs and schedules
- overall, efficient organization so that roles and responsibilities were clearly defined
- good communication between members of the team
- firm commitment by all colleagues to completing the project
- a positive outlook, as demonstrated by seeking realistic solutions to the problems encountered
- successfully dealing with the risks encountered during the project
- the satisfaction of your customers or users and other stakeholders with the outcomes of your project.

A well-costed project

Example of a final statement of income and expenditure for a project to plan a conference

Item	Actual expenditure	Budgeted expenditure	Notes
Speaker	6,100	6,000	1
Venue	5,000	4,800	2
Publicity	2,200	2,400	3
Salaries	120,000	120,000	4
Office equipment	9,000	8,400	5
Other overheads	7,000	6,000	6
Total costs	**£149,300**	**147,600**	
Contingency		15,000	
Overall budget		**£162,600**	

Income: £155,000
Profit: £5,700[7]

Notes

1 The speaker's actual costs were £100 higher than budgeted
2 The overall cost of the venue was £200 higher than budgeted
3 The overall cost of publicity was £200 less than budgeted
4 Expenditure on actual salaries was in line with projected figures
5 Expenditure on office equipment was £600 higher than budgeted
6 Expenditure on other overheads was £1,000 higher than budgeted
7 Profit: Income received £155,000 minus actual expenditure £149,300 = profit of £5,700.

TIP *Remember to check the financial figures to see how actual expenditure compared with the planned expenditure in your original budget.*

The conclusion of this project was that, although certain items of expenditure were higher than originally planned (speaker, venue, office equipment, other overheads) and one was lower (publicity), more than sufficient funds were allocated to the contingency, so that overall the project made a profit.

Wrapping up the project

Once you have evaluated the project, acknowledging its successful aspects and recognizing what you might do differently next time, you can make sure that you feed the information back to the team in the following ways:

● **Acknowledge your team's work**
Before the project team disbands, mark the successful conclusion of your project by some form of celebration that is appropriate to your company or organization. You will want to invite your project sponsor who has believed in the project, your customers or users and other stakeholders. You could, for example, pay for a meal out for all the staff concerned and their partners.

● **Recognize the achievements of individuals**
Show your personal appreciation to the key individuals, affirming their work and the significance of their participation in the project. I personally like to remember to thank support staff such as secretarial and admin staff; and I gave copies of a long-term reference work that I had worked on to outside companies that provided stationery supplies and courier services.

● **Plan future meetings**
If the project has been to install new computer systems, you will want to review these after an agreed period to make sure that they are working as they should and to resolve any issues that occur. Future meetings are also the means to build on the (hopefully good) working relationships you have developed during the project and will provide further opportunities for collaboration.

● **Document lessons learned**
If the costings didn't work out, if communications were weak at certain points, document the reasons. Identify what worked well. Identify what did not go well and consider what measures you will take to avoid making the same mistakes again on future projects. Such documented identification will be helpful for you in further projects that you will manage in the future.

● **Write a report for your sponsor**
Produce a final 'end of project' review and report for your project sponsor. Here, you could summarize the progress of the project, examples of good practice, the lessons learned and any recommendations for the future. Ensure that these are written up and keep your own copy, so that you have a record of measures to be taken to avoid making the same mistakes again.

TIP *If the project has raised wider issues, such as a need for better communications between colleagues in different departments of your company or organization, decide what practical steps you will take to improve this.*

● **Tidy up other 'loose ends'**
There will be some relatively insignificant outstanding issues that you will still need to resolve.

● **Go through the project paperwork**
Now is the time to go through the paperwork you will have amassed during the project. Do not destroy key documents that you might need in the future as evidence of particular decisions, but you can destroy many working documents.

● **Continue to learn**
However many projects you may manage, you will always find more effective ways of achieving your goals.

Summary

Today we have been concerned with the process of concluding and evaluating a project. This process involves checking that you delivered all that you have agreed to, and ensuring that any associated work (such as training new users) is undertaken well. It also means building on the relationships you developed during the life of your project, so that you can discuss its good and not so good points and acknowledge the successes of your and your team's achievements in completing the project. You also learned about the importance of considering the reasons for any mistakes made, and noting them so that you can incorporate them into future working practices.

Now take the following practical steps:

1 Think of the three best things about the project you have just completed.

2 Think of two weaknesses in the project you have just completed.

3 What steps will you take to avoid making these mistakes again?

4 What are you looking forward to in your next project?

5 What are you not looking forward to in your next project?

6 What can you do to minimize any anxiety you might have?

Fact-check [answers at the back]

1. What should happen as your project draws to a close?
   a) You can now slacken your monitoring controls ❑
   b) You can now leave the project ❑
   c) You can now forget your goal ❑
   d) Keep up all your monitoring controls ❑

2. How important is the satisfaction of your customers or end users?
   a) Quite important ❑
   b) Essential ❑
   c) A luxury ❑
   d) Unimportant ❑

3. What should you do when dealing with lessons you have learned?
   a) Discuss them, but don't write them down ❑
   b) Discuss them and write them down, but do nothing about them ❑
   c) Discuss them, write them down and act on them, so that you incorporate them into your working practices ❑
   d) Ignore them, so that you make the same mistakes again ❑

4. How should you deal with a mistake in a project?
   a) Publicly blame the colleague responsible ❑
   b) Privately have a quiet word with the colleague responsible ❑
   c) Ignore the colleague responsible ❑
   d) Talk to everyone about the colleague responsible behind his or her back ❑

5. How important is recognizing personal achievements in a project?
   a) Essential ❑
   b) Desirable ❑
   c) A luxury ❑
   d) A waste of time ❑

6. When evaluating a project, what should you be?
   a) As ingenious as possible ❑
   b) As vague as possible ❑
   c) As specific as possible ❑
   d) As inaccurate as possible ❑

7. When evaluating a project, what should you especially consider?
   a) Your project sponsor ❑
   b) Procedures changed ❑
   c) Holiday taken ❑
   d) Costs and schedules ❑

8. What should the lessons you have learned for future projects be?
   a) Vague and unrealistic ❑
   b) Specific and measurable ❑
   c) Right for everyone else, but not for you ❑
   d) As imaginative as possible ❑

9. What should you do about lessons learned?
   a) Ignore them anyway ❑
   b) Tell your partner at home ❑
   c) Concentrate on several small ones ❑
   d) Concentrate on the few main ones ❑

10. When thinking about your next
project, what should you do?
a) Ignore your failures ❏
b) Pass this book to a colleague ❏
c) Go over this book again ❏
d) Think you know it all, so you
have no need to read this
book again ❏

7 × 7

Seven key ideas

1 Establish a solid plan from the outset: don't rush yourself into starting a project without understanding the goals, challenges and risks.

2 Set a timetable or schedule and share this with the project team: if they don't know their deadlines, they won't be able to stick to them. If necessary, revise the schedule as the project progresses.

3 Use measurable milestones: woolly objectives serve no purpose.

4 Don't underestimate the resources you require: time, budget, personnel – be realistic about all of these during planning rather than repeatedly making special pleadings as the project progresses.

5 Communicate effectively: through meeting, emails and progress reports, ensure that all key stakeholders are in the loop.

6 Confront risks and exploit opportunities.

7 Work out how you will measure quality objectively

Seven great resources

1 The Project Management Institute, a professional project management members organization: www.pmi.org.uk

2 Prince2, a project management methodology and qualification. Courses and downloads available here: www.prince2.com

3 Project Management Tips, a website offering advice and tools: pmtips.net

4 Lynda.com, an online learning company with modules on project management: www.lynda.com

5 Project Smart, exploring trends and developments in project management: www.projectsmart.co.uk

6 Agile, a project management methodology and qualification evolved from software development: www.gov.uk/service-manual/agile

7 Cabinet Office Best Management Practice Portfolio: www.gov.uk/government/publications/best-management-practice-portfolio/about-the-office-of-government-commerce

Seven things to do today

1 Draw a mind map or pattern diagram for your project: write the name of your project in the centre of a sheet of paper and create a spider's web of aspects surrounding it. This is a great way to capture key information about a project.
2 Start a risk register: if you don't already have one, start by identifying situations in the project that could throw a spanner in the works. Rather than ignoring them or hoping they won't happen, assess the risk and allocate an owner to prepare for, monitor and resolve the issue.
3 Get SMART! Start using SMART goals to deliver your project: Specific, Measurable, Agreed, Realistic, Timed. A SMART project manager equals an effective project manager.
4 Catch up on some admin, or remind others to do so. It's inevitable that administrative tasks are pushed aside from time to time, but set aside some quiet time to get on with it.
5 Create a Gantt chart to log your remaining hours and tasks, and who is responsible for completing them.
6 Encourage your team and listen to their concerns: a motivated and well-managed project team will deliver better results.
7 Reread your project plan or initiation documents. Has your project suffered from scope creep, budgeting issues, timing issues, or has anything else gone awry? Has anything gone better than planned and can it be capitalized upon?

Seven things to avoid

1 Don't agree to unrealistic schedule or budget constraints at the beginning of a project. Everyone wants everything faster and cheaper, but you are setting yourself up for disaster if you play down the required resources at the set-up stage.
2 Similarly, set realistic targets for your team. Tough targets are fine – they can 'stretch' colleagues and bring the best out in people – but impossible targets are just that.
3 Don't forge ahead with a project if you are unclear about the goals or expected outcomes. Sometimes these can change during the project's cycle. Check with the stakeholders and project directors if you need confirmation.

4 Be sure to listen! Great communication makes a project run smoothly, and a substantial part of being a good communicator is being a good listener.

5 Don't be an ostrich. Remove your head from the sand and deal with change constructively.

6 Don't lower your quality standards to 'get things done'. In the longer term this will result in more work.

7 Know your limits! Very few projects are achieved by one person. Assemble a good project team and delegate tasks to suitable candidates.

Seven great quotes

1 'All things are created twice; first mentally; then physically. The key to creativity is to begin with the end in mind, with a vision and a blueprint of the desired result.' Stephen Covey (1932–2012), American educator and author

2 'Trying to manage a project without project management is like trying to play a football game without a game plan.' Karen Tate, Board Member, Project Management Institute

3 '"Begin at the beginning," the King said gravely, "and go on till you come to the end; then stop."' *Alice's Adventures in Wonderland*, Lewis Carroll (1832–98)

4 'I will either find a way, or make one.' Attributed to Hannibal (247–182 BCE), when his generals advised him that he could not march an army across the Alps

5 'Why do so many professionals say they are project-managing, when what they are actually doing is fire-fighting?' Colin Bentley, former Chief Examiner for OGC PRINCE2

6 'Everyone needs deadlines.' Walt Disney (1901–66)

7 'Planning is everything, the plan is nothing.' President Dwight Eisenhower (1890–1969)

Seven questions to always ask

1 Why?
2 How?
3 What?
4 Who?
5 When?
6 Where?
7 How much?

Seven ways to future-proof your PM skills

1 Aim for qualifications: in recent years, more project-management methodologies and qualifications have been developed. Potential employers like to see practical experience backed up with certificates.

2 Get used to using project-management programs. The days of hand-drawn flowcharts and wall planners are going the way of the dinosaurs: familiarize yourself with programs such as Visio, Excel, PowerPoint, and understand the basics of CMS programs.

3 Manage risks effectively: 'risk management' is a buzzword in project management; while software can help you to identify risks, the way you choose to resolve them will play a significant part in your future.

4 Promote quality: the way isn't to cut corners on quality just to achieve results quickly. Good project management will always be about reviewing and providing quality.

5 Be cyber-secure! Most future projects will be computer-based, and guarding the project's cycle and conclusion from outsiders will become an important part of the project manager's portfolio.

6 Stay mobile. Project management will no longer be confined to a tower PC at a desk: get used to using mobile technology to coordinate your team and project. 2014 saw mobile internet usage outstrip PC usage for the first time in history and that trend is set to continue.

7 Continue to communicate: technology and telecoms are there to make this easier, but at the heart of a well-run project is a project manager with effective communication skills.

Answers

Sunday: 1b; 2d; 3c; 4c; 5a; 6b; 7c; 8d; 9a; 10b

Monday: 1d; 2c; 3a; 4d; 5a; 6b; 7c; 8a; 9d; 10c

Tuesday: 1c; 2d; 3d; 4b; 5d; 6b; 7c; 8c; 9a; 10b

Wednesday: 1d; 2c; 3a; 4d; 5d; 6c; 7c; 8d; 9c; 10b

Thursday: 1b; 2d; 3b; 4b; 5c; 6c; 7d; 8a; 9d; 10b

Friday: 1b; 2b; 3c; 4a; 5d; 6b; 7d; 8c; 9d; 10c

Saturday: 1d; 2b; 3c; 4b; 5a; 6c; 7d; 8b; 9d; 10c

61-67